BACKROADS

—— *of* ——

NEW YORK

BACKROADS

——— *of* ———

NEW YORK

*Your Guide to New York's Most
Scenic Backroad Adventures*

TEXT BY **KIM KNOX BECKIUS**
PHOTOGRAPHY BY **CARL E. HEILMAN II**

Voyageur Press

DEDICATION

To my mother and father, who instilled in me a love of travel and exploring,
and to my wife, Meg, who has always been there to support my dreams.
— CEH

To my husband, Bruce—researcher, driver, and awesome snack packer
— KKB

First published in 2007 by Voyageur Press, an imprint of MBI Publishing Company, Galtier Plaza, Suite 200, 380 Jackson Street, St. Paul, MN 55101 USA

The information in this book is true and complete to the best of our knowledge. All recommendations are made without any guarantee on the part of the author or Publisher, who also disclaim any liability incurred in connection with the use of this data or specific details.

We recognize, further, that some words, model names, and designations mentioned herein are the property of the trademark holder. We use them for identification purposes only. This is not an official publication.

Voyageur Press titles are also available at discounts in bulk quantity for industrial or sales-promotional use. For details write to Special Sales Manager at MBI Publishing Company, Galtier Plaza, Suite 200, 380 Jackson Street, St. Paul, MN 55101 USA

To find out more about our books, join us online at www.voyageurpress.com.

Library of Congress Cataloging-in-Publication Data

Beckius, Kim Knox.
  Backroads of New York : your guide to New York's most scenic backroad adventures / text by Kim Knox Beckius; photography by Carl E. Heilman II.
      p. cm.
  Includes bibliographical references and index.
  ISBN-13: 978-0-7603-2955-9 (softbound)
  ISBN-10: 0-7603-2955-9 (softbound)
  1. New York (State)—Guidebooks. 2. Automobile travel—New York (State) 3. Scenic byways—New York (State)—Guidebooks. I. Title.
F117.3.B43 2007
917.47'0444—dc22
                                    2006038827

Editor: Josh Leventhal
Designer: Brenda C. Canales
Maps by Mary Firth

Printed in China

ON THE FRONT COVER: The Bear Mountain Bridge and Bear Mountain State Park in autumn.
ON THE SPINE: Fort Ontario State Historic Site, with the Oswego West Pierhead Lighthouse in the background.
ON THE BACK COVER: *(above)* Robert G. Wehle State Park, overlooking Lake Ontario. *(bottom left)* Clermont State Historic Site, Columbia County; *(bottom right)* State Route 52 winding throught the Shawangunks above Ellenville.
ON THE TITLE PAGE: Lake George and Buck Mountain, as viewed from Prospect Mountain.
ON THE TITLE PAGE, INSET: Allegany State Park in autumn.

CONTENTS

INTRODUCTION

ABOVE:
Camp Sagamore has been welcoming vacationers looking for a rustic, yet elegant, Adirondack experience since the turn of the twentieth century.

FACING PAGE:
Scenic farmlands, such as this one just north of Lyons Falls in Lewis County, are encountered on backroads throughout the state of New York.

New York City's Times Square is often called the "crossroads of the world." Leave the flash, dazzle, and frenetic pace of Manhattan behind, though, and you'll soon discover that the backroads of New York State lead to even more diversity than can be claimed by that urban island.

New York is simultaneously a place of vaulted peaks and rolling farmlands, of sophisticated suburbs and backwoods towns, of coastal sanctuaries juxtaposed with exclusive seaside communities. The state owes its richly varied landscape to ancient geologic events, but it is those whose lives have played out against this alluring backdrop who have infused each region, and indeed each city and town, with distinct character.

You can travel from the Big Apple to Buffalo in about six-and-a-half hours on the New York State Thruway, or you can spend a lifetime exploring the thoroughfares and country lanes that reveal New York's multifaceted personality. We hope this book will inspire you to do the latter. Maps, directions, and travel tips will guide you to both legendary and little-known places, while vivid images will whet your appetite for adventure.

New York's story is one of human ambition, and these drives will allow you to discover the contributions of successive generations. You'll walk on sacred battlegrounds, tour millionaires' mansions and Underground Railroad stops, and visit the spot where women first proclaimed their equality. You'll also be charmed by quirky monuments to human endeavor, like the Jell-O Museum in LeRoy, or the Desilu Playhouse in Lucille Ball's hometown, where carefully reconstructed sets immerse you in the comedic world of the Ricardos.

While each of these suggested trips can be completed in a day, you'll want to allow more time if you plan to make every stop and hike every trail. Remember that as seasons change, so do the activities you can pursue and the scenes you'll view. New York, which has twice hosted the winter Olympics, is renowned for its snow sports. The sugar maple is the state tree, and late February through early April is the time to see syrup-making demonstrations at rural sugarhouses. As the snow melts in the spring, waterfalls and rivers are at their most vigorous. Crisp mountain air and tranquil lakes lure summer vacationers, but be prepared to battle black flies in the Adirondacks in late May and June. The Hudson Valley and Catskill Mountains are truly a sight to behold when cloaked in the ambers, reds, and oranges of autumn. And the holiday season is a special time to visit the Finger Lakes village of Seneca Falls, which inspired the setting for Frank Capra's classic film, *It's a Wonderful Life*. Whatever your passion, memorable experiences await within New York's borders.

Use these suggested routes as a starting point, but don't be afraid to allow spontaneity to alter your itinerary. Even in the most remote regions, you'll spot roadside markers that will tempt you to tarry. Before you set out, invest in a New York road atlas and a compass. You may also want to pack snacks. One thing you won't find easily once you leave the bright lights of the big city behind is a slice of pizza at midnight.

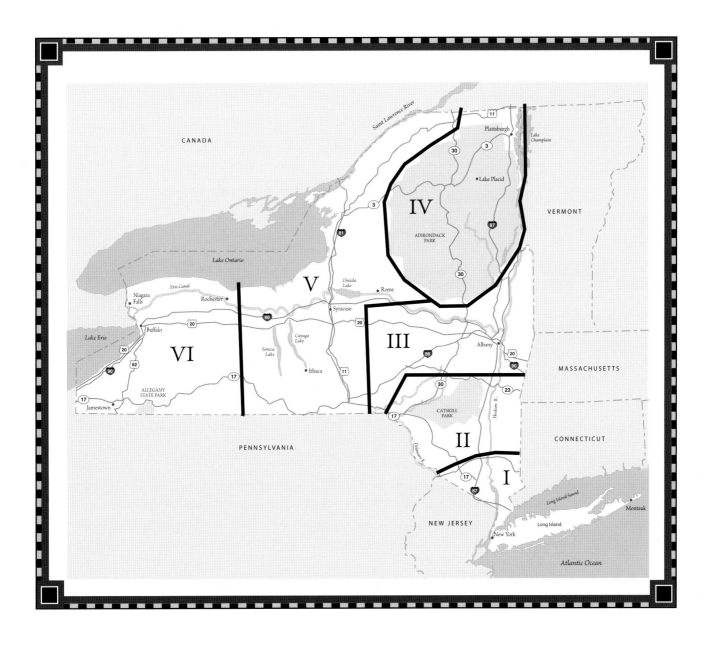

PART I

CITY OUTSKIRTS
SAME SOPHISTICATION, DIFFERENT SPEED

ABOVE:
A visit to West Point offers a glimpse into the life of today's cadets, who follow in the proud tradition of such notable graduates as Ulysses S. Grant, Robert E. Lee, Jefferson Davis, and Dwight D. Eisenhower.

FACING PAGE:
The Bear Mountain Bridge spans a scenic stretch of the Hudson River, in the southern Hudson Highlands.

There are two New Yorks. One is the city, the largest metropolitan area in the nation, the place where a minute flashes by in less than sixty seconds and careers are made and destroyed overnight. What happens in Gotham (as the city was nicknamed by Washington Irving) has global reverberations, whether it's a deal struck on Wall Street or a design paraded down a runway.

Surprisingly, though, one needn't venture far off Broadway to see that New York, the state, shuns much of the frenzy and glitz of its namesake city. You'll find New York's sprawling suburbs sophisticated, yet surprisingly scenic; percolating, yet delightfully placid. Within footsteps of commuter rail stations lie natural refuges of superb beauty, wild landscapes forever preserved, and historic places where legends live on.

Of course, the city's influence is omnipresent, whether you're peering at the price tags in a boutique in the Hamptons, listening to world-class opera in an open-air theater, or squinting at the Manhattan skyline from the summit of Bear Mountain. And yet, as you spy an osprey circling its nest, ride merrily 'round on a carousel skunk, watch Shakespearean drama unfolding under the stars, or stomp freshly harvested grapes, you'll definitely get your sixty seconds out of every minute—maybe more.

OUTER LONG ISLAND
NEW YORK'S CAPE

ROUTE 1

From Orient Point, follow New York State Route 25 West to a left on State Route 114 South in Greenport. Take the Shelter Island North Ferry and continue to follow Route 114 South as it winds across the island to the South Ferry entrance. When you reach North Haven on the opposite shore, follow Route 114 South once again to a right on State Route 27 West, then a left on James Lane. Return to Route 27 and proceed east to a right on Old Montauk Highway, which follows the shore. In Montauk, return to Route 27 East, which ends at Montauk Point.

Two boroughs of America's largest city are actually located on the largest island of the continental United States. Separated from Manhattan by the East River, Long Island is home to more than 4.7 million New Yorkers who live in Brooklyn and Queens. Travel to the eastern extremities of this narrow, 118-mile appendage of the big city, though, and you'll discover a coastal refuge that is more sleepy New England than insomniac metropolis.

If you arrive in Orient Point on Long Island's North Fork via ferry from New London, Connecticut, the transition to historic whaling towns, waterfront parks, and narrow streets lined with farm stands and shingled homes will be less abrupt than if you've fled Manhattan. Western Long Island was originally part of the Connecticut colony, and the North Fork has ancient geologic ties to its northern neighbor. It helped to contain the former freshwater Lake Connecticut, formed as the last glacier melted ten thousand years ago. One sniff inside Orient Beach State Park, however, and you'll know the tides eventually tore through the outer rim, allowing the ocean's salty flow to transform the vast lake into Long Island Sound.

The 357-acre Orient Beach State Park is more than a summer beach haven and prime saltwater fishing spot. Its marshes are breeding grounds for heron, egret, and ospreys, and its rare maritime forest is home to red cedar and black-jack oak trees, as well as prickly pear cacti that bloom in early July.

Charming Greenport is a former whaling town, with sea captains' Victorian homes now welcoming overnight guests and tall-masted

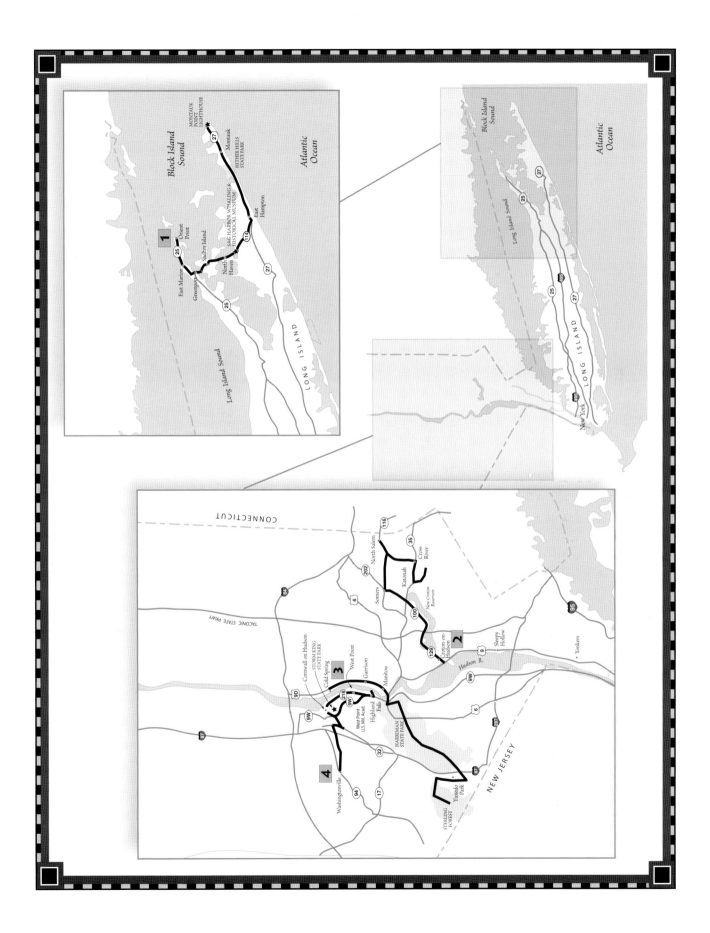

Nearly one-third of the ecologically delicate Shelter Island is within the confines of The Nature Conservancy's Mashomack Preserve.

Osprey nesting platforms are a common sight on Outer Long Island; spring is the best season to see these raptors in protective flight over their roosts.

Although the sun has set on Sag Harbor's days as a busy commercial port, this charming, deepwater harbor continues to beckon to pleasure boaters.

Authorized in 1792 by the Second Congress under George Washington, the Montauk Point Lighthouse continues to guide ships around the tip of Long Island.

schooners departing for sightseeing sails. First settled in 1682, and a railroad stop since 1844, the town is home to a branch of the Railroad Museum of Long Island, located in an old freight house adjacent to the Long Island Railroad station. Those with an interest in maritime history should visit the East End Seaport Museum at the ferry dock, which houses a small collection of boats, tools, art, and artifacts. Children will want to try to grasp a brass ring and win another spin on Greenport's historic 1920s carousel, sheltered inside a glass roundhouse in Mitchell Park.

From Greenport, you can travel by ferry to the isle the Manhanset Indians called *Manhansack-aha-quashawomock*, or "island sheltered by islands." The first English settlers, including Quaker refugees from Massachusetts, arrived on Shelter Island in the 1650s, and some of their descendants still inhabit this tall isle tucked within the protective embrace of Long Island's North and South Forks. The island has a 35-mile-per-hour speed limit, so you'll have to wriggle slowly southward on twisting Route 114, past homes representing many architectural periods, an old Quaker cemetery, and the town hall, where you can purchase a parking permit if you want to visit island beaches. Before you reach the South Ferry, which will take you off "the Rock," watch for the entrance to Mashomack Preserve on the left. The Nature Conservancy purchased this 2,100-acre property to ensure protection of the diverse and scenic habitat of the East Coast's densest population of nesting ospreys and, at times, endangered piping plovers and least terns. A handicap-accessible, mile-long boardwalk provides a glimpse of this unique environment, and four longer trails offer deeper access for those who like to hike.

The Hamptons await as you return to land, head south, and then east along Long Island's South Fork. The region's reputation as a tony playground for the city's elite is well-deserved, but as you journey through the towns of Sag Harbor and East Hampton, you'll discover that underneath the surface of posh shops, pricey restaurants, and private beaches lies intriguing history. Walk along Sag Harbor's Long Wharf or visit the Sag Harbor Whaling and Historical Museum on Main Street, and you'll learn how the town's deep harbor made it a vibrant seaport from the early seventeenth century until 1847, when whaling activity peaked. Sag Harbor was named the state's official port of entry in 1789 and continued to rival New York City as a center of seagoing commerce until the mid-eighteenth century. The village of East Hampton—with its three historic, English-style windmills—was laid out in the form of a New England agricultural plantation when it was established in 1648 by settlers from Connecticut and Massachusetts. If you doubt that there is anything humble about the Hamptons, visit the Home Sweet Home Museum on James Lane, the childhood residence of accomplished actor, dramatist, and poet John Howard Payne, who penned the timeless lyrics: "Be it ever so humble, there's no place like home."

Even if you can't afford a humble home in the Hamptons, the proliferation of public parks in the hamlet of Montauk, located on New

Colonel Teddy Roosevelt and the Rough Riders rest at Montauk Point after their return from Cuba in August 1898. The Granger Collection, New York

York's easternmost point, ensures that a glimpse of the good life is available to all. Amble along Napeague Bay's parabolic-shaped and ever-evolving "walking dunes" or sleep under the stars in Hither Hills State Park. Frolic in the surf or poke around two concrete World War II bunkers at Shadmoor State Park. Obtain a fishing permit and try surfcasting at the former air force station that is now part of Camp Hero State Park. Reserve a trusty mount at Deep Hollow Ranch, and go horseback riding on the beach at Theodore Roosevelt County Park, site of America's first cattle ranch. Theodore "Teddy" Roosevelt and his Rough Riders recuperated here after their charge up San Juan Hill during the Spanish-American War.

Or, if you, too, could simply use a restful afternoon with a scenic view, head straight out to Montauk Point State Park, where the brown-and-white Montauk Point Lighthouse has stood guard since 1796. New York's oldest lighthouse, it is sometimes open for tours. Look closely offshore, and you'll be able to watch the race of tides converging from the Atlantic Ocean and Block Island Sound. It's nothing like the rat race of the big city, and as Hamptons homeowner Martha Stewart would say, that's "a good thing."

WESTCHESTER COUNTY
CITY MEETS COUNTRY

New York City may be known as the city that never sleeps, but those who have earned their fame and fortune there do occasionally need some shuteye. Westchester County has a reputation for being the crash pad for those who move and shake the world by day. But while it may have the state's densest concentration of country clubs and sprawling, multimillion-dollar estates, Westchester is inviting to all who seek the divine combination of cultural sophistication and a breath of fresh air.

ROUTE 2

From Croton Point Park in Croton-on-Hudson, follow Croton Point Avenue to a right turn onto South Riverside Avenue to Van Cortlandt Manor. Backtrack on South Riverside Avenue to a right on New York State Route 129 East. Proceed straight onto Route 118 South. At the end, turn left onto State Route 100 North. Shortly after it becomes U.S. Route 202 East in Somers, turn right onto State Route 116. Watch for turns to stay on Route 116. Turn left onto June Road, then right on Deveau Road to visit the Hammond Museum and Japanese Stroll Garden. Continue north on June Road to a left on Hardscrabble Road and the North Salem Vineyard. Return to June Road and drive south to a left on Route 116 East, then turn right on State Route 121 South. Turn right onto State Route 35 West, then left onto State Route 22 South. Bear left onto Girdle Ridge Road.

ABOVE: *Located on the Hudson River within walking distance of the Croton-Harmon Train Station, Croton Point Park is popular for its beach and camping facilities in the summer and eagle-spotting opportunities in the winter.*

RIGHT: *Guides in Federal-period costume lead tours of Van Cortlandt Manor, providing a glimpse of the lifestyle of one of New York's most prominent families in the years just after the Revolutionary War.*

The New Croton Dam is an engineering wonder and reportedly the world's second largest hand-hewn stone structure, after Egypt's Great Pyramids.

The village of Croton-on-Hudson, which lies thirty miles north of Manhattan at the confluence of the Croton and Hudson Rivers, is an ideal point of departure for discovering the "city meets country" allure of northern Westchester. Croton Point, a county park located on a 508-acre peninsula jutting into the Hudson, was home to the Kitchawanc tribe when Dutch traders arrived in the 1600s. During the Revolutionary War, when two local militiamen spotted a British sloop moored off Croton Point, they borrowed a cannon and forced the ship to flee. Little did they know they had struck an important blow. Without a getaway sloop, British spy John André was captured, and his conspiracy to capture West Point with Benedict Arnold's treasonous aid was thwarted. Along the park's Discovery Trail are vestiges of America's first wine cellar, built in 1827 when the Underhill family operated a vineyard on the point.

Although its economy was primarily agricultural, Westchester was the richest county in the colony by 1775. Most of northern Westchester was contained within the 86,000-acre manor granted in 1697 to the politically prominent Van Cortlandt family. The family's beer-brewing operations in New York City generated great wealth, and commercial development and tenant farming made its Westchester estate prosperous. At Van Cortlandt Manor, visitors can tour the manor house, which contains many original furnishings; a reconstructed tenant house, where cooking, spinning, and weaving demonstrations are conducted; and the Ferry House, a rural tavern built before 1750.

As you drive east along Route 129, the entrance to Croton Gorge Park comes up quickly on the right. Here, you'll see the New Croton Dam, with its distinctive stepped spillway. Built between 1892 and 1907, primarily by Italian immigrants, the dam controls the flow of water from the thirty-four-billion-gallon Croton Reservoir, which collects fresh water for New York City. The twenty-six-mile Old Croton Aqueduct Trail—a footpath atop the masonry tunnel that provided Manhattan with its first reliable water source beginning in 1842—is accessible from the park for those interested in a leisurely walk to the Bronx.

If you'd rather see horses than hoof it, continue on to Muscoot Farm on Route 100 in Somers. The Hopkins family, whose fortune flowed from Ferdinand T. Hopkins' invention of Mother Sill's Seasick Remedy, operated the farm from 1880 until 1967, originally as a gentleman's farm. It later became a more serious dairying operation. Today, it is a county park open free to the public year-round. You'll see original buildings, including the dairy barn, ice house, and blacksmith shop, and rare twentieth-century livestock breeds. What you won't see is an elephant.

You will, however, see the Elephant Hotel just before you leave Somers on the way to North Salem. The hotel, now the Somers Town Hall, was built in 1824 by Hachaliah Bailey to honor "Old Bet," one of the first elephants in America. Bailey intended to use the pachyderm for farm labor, but he soon found that exhibiting her throughout the Northeast was a surer ticket to riches. Somers was christened the "cradle of the American circus," as neighbors and relatives envious of Bailey's success began touring with their own exotic menageries.

The circus can certainly be considered an art form, but art of a more contemplative and cultivated nature awaits in North Salem. East and West intermingle at the Hammond Museum and Japanese Stroll Garden, where exhibitions, performances, and classes blend cultures and artistic traditions. Open seasonally, the museum and its tranquil gardens are a place to revere beauty in both natural and fabricated forms. Nearby, North Salem Vineyard is the only winery in Westchester that grows its own grapes. It is open for tours and tastings on weekends year-round. After a few sips of refreshing Seyval Blanc, you'll be ready to continue to Katonah, a hamlet of Bedford with an intriguing history.

In 1897, determined to preserve their community in the face of New York City's decision to flood Katonah to create the Croton Reservoir, residents used draft horses to pull fifty-five buildings along soap-slicked timber tracks to a new upland location. As you explore Katonah's attractions, you'll have another opportunity to appreciate Westchester's rustic urbanity. The changing exhibits in the galleries and outdoor sculpture park of the Katonah Museum of Art on Route 22 are fresh and evocative.

Just up the road, the John Jay Homestead State Historic Site preserves the agrarian way of life that was cherished by the nation's first chief justice. After an impressive political career, Jay retired to the farm that was purchased by his grandfather, Jacobus Van Cortlandt, in 1703. Today, visitors can explore the Federal-period farmhouse, farm buildings, schoolhouse, and gardens on the property.

Wend your way, finally, to Caramoor on Girdle Ridge Road. This ninety-acre property, with its nine enchanting gardens and treasure-filled house museum, is home to New York's largest outdoor music festival. Walter and Lucie Rosen bequeathed their estate and its Mediterranean-style palazzo to create a center for music and the arts. Caramoor draws internationally acclaimed performers every summer. New York City may have Carnegie Hall, but at Caramoor, the music is superb, the setting is exquisite, and the parking is free.

THE LOWER HUDSON VALLEY
RIVER TIDES AND MOUNTAINSIDES

In the Algonquin language, the Hudson River was called *Muhheakunnuk*, or "river that flows two ways." As far north as the city of Troy, 153 miles inland, the river is a tidal estuary, where saline Atlantic Ocean droplets mix with freshwater flowing from the Hudson's headwaters in the Adirondacks. When oceans probe inland, the varying environmental conditions that are created foster disparate and abundant life. The Lower Hudson Valley's natural riches fueled Manhattan's rise, but by the turn of the twentieth century, logging and quarrying had destroyed important habitats and much of the region's intrinsic beauty. The damage, however, was not irreversible.

ROUTE 3

From the village of Cold Spring, follow New York State Route 301 to State Route 9D South. Follow U.S. Route 6 West across the Bear Mountain Bridge and pick up U.S. Route 9W South from the traffic circle. Turn right on the park entrance road to enter Bear Mountain State Park. At Bear Mountain Circle, pick up Seven Lakes Drive. Turn right on Perkins Memorial Drive to the summit of Bear Mountain. Descend and turn right, continuing on Seven Lakes Drive to U.S. 6 West. Take exit 18 on U.S. 6, and from the traffic circle, pick up Seven Lakes Drive once again through Harriman State Park. Turn right on State Route 17 North, then left on State Route 17A West. Turn left onto Long Meadow Road, then bear right onto Old Forge Road to Sterling Forest State Park.

Breakneck Ridge and Storm King Mountain, which mark the gateway to the Hudson Highlands, come into view as a replica of the Half Moon *retraces Henry Hudson's historic 1609 voyage.*

When Boscobel opened to the public in 1961, Governor Nelson A. Rockefeller called it "one of the most beautiful homes ever built in America."

Incorporated in 1846, the charming riverside village of Cold Spring retains an aura of yesteryear; more than a dozen antique shops add to its allure.

It's hard to resist tapping the brakes as you cross the mighty Hudson on the Bear Mountain Bridge. You may even want to walk across the bridge, as Appalachian Trail hikers do when they cross the Hudson en route from Georgia to Maine.

Dogwood trees blossom in Bear Mountain State Park each spring, and soon Hessian Lake will be dotted with paddleboats and rowboats.

A postcard view of the Bear Mountain Bridge over the Hudson River, from shortly after the bridge's completion.

Some of New York's most dramatic achievements in historic preservation and wilderness reclamation are found along this drive in the Hudson Highlands. The tour begins at Cold Spring, a former foundry town noted for its nineteenth-century architecture and now a National Historic District. Situated at the river's edge, the village is home to antique shops, boutiques, and cafés.

Nearby on Route 9D, Boscobel is an architectural jewel and a testament to those who fought for and financed its rescue. This Federal-style mansion was built between 1804 and 1808 by the Dyckman family. When you see Boscobel's graceful façade, it may surprise you to learn that the home was actually constructed about fifteen miles away, in Montrose. Slated for demolition in the 1950s, it was acquired by preservation-minded residents, who dismantled and stored the home. In 1956, Lila Acheson Wallace, who founded *Reader's Digest* with her husband, donated funds to purchase the waterfront property in Garrison, where Boscobel was carefully reconstructed. The home, open April through December, is furnished with period pieces. The equally lovely grounds host the Hudson Valley Shakespeare Festival each summer.

Just past Boscobel, watch for a right turn onto Indian Brook Road, a dirt road that leads to the visitors' center at Constitution Marsh Audubon Center and Sanctuary. Within this 270-acre wetland, rare birds breed, and plants and animals native to the Hudson River estuary thrive. A half-mile hike leads to a seven-hundred-foot boardwalk that extends into the marsh. Even if you're not a birder, artist, or photographer, you'll enjoy the unique experience of being dwarfed by gently swaying cattails and tall grasses, as you are immersed in the subtle hum of life within this vital ecosystem.

Continue along Route 9D to the left-hand entrance for Manitoga/The Russel Wright Design Center, where you'll see the wonder that emerges when nature gets an assist from an artist. Noted industrial designer Russel Wright purchased this abandoned quarry in 1942, gave it the Algonquin name that means "place of the great spirit," and set to work transforming the seventy-five-acre wasteland into a dream environment, replanted with native trees, ferns, and wildflowers. Four miles of paths wind through this woodland landscape, and Dragon Rock—the intriguing home that Wright built on the quarry ledge—overlooks a pond and waterfall. Tours of the structure, which has a century-old cedar tree as its main support, are available seasonally by reservation.

The Bear Mountain Bridge, which you'll encounter en route to Bear Mountain State Park, was also designed to blend with its surroundings.

You will cross the river in minutes, but in 1913, when the state park opened and a million visitors arrived annually, the wait for a ferry to Bear Mountain was often as long as four hours. The steel suspension bridge opened to traffic in 1924 and was the first permanent Hudson River crossing south of Albany and the longest span of its type at the time. Its engineering successes influenced the design of many other bridges, including San Francisco's Golden Gate Bridge.

Located only fifty miles from New York City, the 5,067-acre Bear Mountain State Park remains an incredibly popular destination. The state's plan to relocate Sing Sing Prison to Bear Mountain in 1909 prompted wealthy landowners, led by railroad tycoon E. H. Harriman and his wife, Mary, to donate lands and funds to save the region from development. Picturesque in winter—when cross-country skiers glide along trails, skaters crowd the rink, and those averse to cold sip cocoa inside the rustic 1915 Bear Mountain Inn—the park is even more resplendent, albeit crowded, in summer. Visitors can swim in the pool, rent paddleboats on Hessian Lake, visit the wildlife rehabilitation center at the Trailside Museums, hike many paths (including a segment of the Appalachian Trail), or ride the only carousel in the world with a bobcat, turkey, bear, deer, and skunk prancing among the ponies.

On busy summer weekends, you may want to simply drive through the park and head to the summit of Bear Mountain. A climb up Perkins Memorial Tower yields panoramic views of the Hudson, surrounding peaks, and the Manhattan skyline. Continue following Seven Lakes Drive, and you'll enter the adjacent 46,647-acre Harriman State Park. New York's second largest state park contains thirty-one lakes and reservoirs, two hundred miles of trails, three beaches, and two campgrounds.

With such fine facilities, even this enormous tract of land can seem cramped at peak times, so if you yearn for a quiet, pristine setting, press on to Sterling Forest State Park, the 17,719-acre refuge next door. Trails here include several short, half-mile hikes and a self-guided, 1.7-mile exploration of the remains of the Sterling Iron Works, North America's first iron mining and processing operation. From the early 1700s until the early 1900s, 1.2 million tons of magnetite ore were extracted from this site to create everything from tools and farm implements, to Revolutionary War cannonballs and the Great Chain that blocked British ships from sailing upriver in 1778.

The state's acquisition of Sterling Forest in 1998 and adjacent lands in 2002 forged the final link in a chain of green that is vital to New York's future. Once so polluted it was referred to as an "open sewer" by a presidential council, the Hudson River is now one of the healthiest estuaries on the Atlantic seaboard. Its rising and falling tides may be imperceptible to those who drive along its banks, but the tidal shift in public opinion that favored preservation over commercialization is readily evident to anyone who explores the wild, open spaces along the Hudson's lush mountainsides.

Along the Storm King Highway, stone walls are all that seemingly stand between drivers and the Hudson River, two hundred feet below.

From Trophy Point on the grounds of the United States Military Academy, it's easy to see how wise George Washington was to stake out this location high above the Hudson for America's defenses.

The nonprofit Bannerman Castle Trust is actively raising funds to stabilize and restore the renowned ruins on Pollopel Island, which is owned by the New York State Office of Parks, Recreation and Historic Preservation.

ROUTE 4

From Brotherhood Winery in Washingtonville, follow New York State Route 94 North to a right on Orrs Mills Road. At the end, turn right on State Route 32 South, then turn left on Angola Road/County Road 65 in Mountainville. Turn left at a stop sign to continue on Angola Road. Turn right and follow U.S. Route 9W South to the second exit for West Point/Highland Falls. Proceed through the village of Highland Falls to the United States Military Academy's Thayer Gate. Return to U.S. 9W North, then turn right to pick up State Route 218 North/Old Storm King Highway to Cornwall-on-Hudson.

By 1810, New York City's population had reached 96,373, but when John Jacques opened his boot and shoe shop in Little York in 1809, the tiny village, located an hour's drive north of Manhattan, had only nine homes. Thirty years later, Jacques started another business that still draws visitors to the town, renamed Washingtonville in honor of the first president, who once stopped here to water his horse. George Washington, who backed two unsuccessful vineyards close to his Virginia home, would be pleased that Jacques' winegrowing venture has endured since 1839, making Washingtonville home to the oldest continuously operated winery in America. Brotherhood Winery, a National Historic Landmark, survived Prohibition by making wines for religious sacraments. Visitors can learn about the wine- and champagne-making processes; tour the nation's largest underground wine cellar; sample Brotherhood's varietal, sparkling, seasonal, and dessert wines; and even stomp grapes on fall weekends.

Of course, moderation is key if you plan to put your keys in the ignition and set out from Washingtonville to see sights the first commander in chief would still recognize, along with some he could have never envisioned. As you drive along Orrs Mills Road, you'll pass the Denning House, built in 1770 and purchased by William Denning, who welcomed his friend Washington here on several occasions. The house is now owned by an antiquarian book dealer.

Soon, however, the tree-lined road will carry you underneath an engineering marvel that would make ol' George rub his eyes. The Moodna Viaduct was built between 1906 and 1908 by the Erie & Jersey Railroad to carry trains over Moodna Creek. The 3,200-foot-long, 193-foot-tall aerial track was designed to offer minimal wind resistance. From certain vantage points, trains steaming across the viaduct appear to soar against a panoramic mountain backdrop.

Before the end of Orrs Mills Road, turn right on Old Pleasant Hill Road and make your way to another very modern installation superimposed on a scene of natural splendor. The Storm King Art Center is a five-hundred-acre outdoor sculpture park founded in 1960. Whether you walk or take a tram, you'll enjoy the more than 120 enormous, abstract works of contemporary sculpture, most of which are composed of welded steel and framed by even more imposing mountains. Among the collection are creations by David Smith, Alexander Calder, Henry Moore, Louise Nevelson, and other American and European sculptors, each carefully positioned within this seasonally evolving, sunlit gallery.

Backroads lead to U.S. Route 9W, which will take you south to West Point. General Washington selected this wide promontory overlooking a narrow, S-shaped curve in the Hudson River for important fortifications built in 1778. It was here that America's most infamous turncoat fell from grace. Shortly after he was appointed commander of West Point in 1780, Benedict Arnold's devious plot to turn over the fortifications to the British in exchange for £20,000 was uncovered. Arnold fled when he learned of the capture of his co-conspirator;

British intelligence chief, John André, was not as lucky.

With the opening on July 4, 1802, of the nation's first service academy, West Point's scenic and strategic location was assured a lasting place in American military history. The West Point Museum, which showcases two centuries of militaria—from Washington's pistols to Vietnam jungle fatigues—is open free to the public year-round. The museum is adjacent to the visitors' center, from which West Point Tours Inc. offers the only sightseeing access to the 16,000-acre United States Military Academy. Regularly departing bus tours take you to such landmarks as the parade grounds, where Washington once drilled American forces; the 1910 Cadet Chapel, which houses the world's largest church organ; the Old Cadet Chapel erected in 1836; the Post Cemetery, final resting place for five thousand fallen heroes; and magnificent Trophy Point, where you'll see monuments, cannons, and other war relics. Included are several links from the five-hundred-yard, eighty-ton Great Chain that was strung across the Hudson, from West Point to Constitution Island, in 1778 as a deterrent to British warships.

The Moodna Viaduct remains the highest and longest railroad trestle east of the Mississippi River.
Library of Congress

As you head back north, opt for State Route 218 instead of U.S. 9W, as long as conditions aren't too treacherous. The two roads encircle Storm King State Park, a 1,900-acre mountain wilderness where hikers are warned not to wander off trails, because unexploded ordnance remains from days when West Point cadets used an adjacent area for artillery practice. Route 218, also called Storm King Highway, is a jagged gash blasted in 1922 along the granite face of Storm King Mountain. This cliff-hugging course affords breathtaking views of the Hudson River, narrow and fjord-like here, and of Breakneck Mountain on the opposite shore.

Thanks to preservationists' efforts, Washington would still find the glacier-rounded peaks of the Hudson Highlands familiar. The Scottish-style castle out on Pollopel Island, however, might shock the man who refused to be crowned America's first king. Bannerman's Castle, which you'll see as Route 218 descends toward the village of Cornwall-on-Hudson, wasn't a palatial residence, though. It was a warehouse—albeit an elaborate and fanciful one—built between 1901 and 1918 by Francis Bannerman VI to store inventory for his Brooklyn-based military surplus business. Emblazoned "Bannerman's Castle" and visible to travelers passing on boats and trains, it was also a giant billboard.

PART II

THE CATSKILLS AND THE HUDSON VALLEY
CELEBRATED LANDSCAPES

ABOVE:
Stone mile-markers, still visible along U.S. Route 9, indicated to postal carriers on the Albany to New York Post Road how much of their trip remained.

FACING PAGE:
Pigments on canvas will never quite capture the immutable beauty of the billowy Catskill Mountains standing sentry over the Hudson River on a rosy autumn morning.

Until Thomas Cole took his sketchbook into the Catskill wilderness and returned to his easel, inspired to paint radiant mountainscapes and stirring river scenes, artists felt bound to travel to Europe for scenery worthy of their labors. A decade after his first visit to the Catskills in 1825, Cole explained in his "Essay on American Scenery," published in *American Magazine*, that while these peaks may not rival the Alps for altitude, they have "varied, undulating, and exceedingly beautiful outlines. They heave from the valley of the Hudson like the subsiding billows of the ocean after a storm."

Cole's works, and those of his prolific friends, students, and admirers—who came to be known as the Hudson River School of painters, even though they fanned out to capture landscapes from sea to shining sea—inspired a newfound appreciation for the young nation's scenic grandeur. As your backroads journeys in this region take you alongside sparkling ribbons of blue, over densely forested ridges, down historic avenues, and through bucolic farmlands, you'll discover that these scenes, which inspired the nation's first native school of art, later attracted America's rich and famous. The country's movers and shakers vacationed at gracious mountain resorts and built homes with priceless river and mountain views. Even the nation's most tested president, Franklin Delano Roosevelt, and his globe-trotting First Lady returned to the Hudson's shores for respite.

Nor will it seem anything but apropos that while he was painting his earliest Catskills scenes, Cole's other favored subject was Eden.

THE UPPER DELAWARE RIVER VALLEY
ENJOY THE RIDE

ROUTE 5

Follow U.S. Route 6 West through Port Jervis to a left on U.S. 6 West and State Route 209 South/Pike Street to the Port Jervis Turntable. Make a U-turn to follow Routes 6 East and 209 North to a left on New York State Route 97 North. Turn right on County Road 168 in Minisink Ford to visit the Minisink Battleground Park. Return to Route 97 North and turn left immediately onto State Route 590, crossing Roebling's Delaware Aqueduct. Return to Route 97 and continue north to Hancock.

Even if there were no hallowed battlegrounds to walk, no engineering marvels to see, no reconstructed Colonial forts to tour, and no raptors swooping overhead, Route 97 from Port Jervis to Hancock would be worth the drive. The creation of this seventy-one-mile roadway, which mirrors the tortuous course of the Upper Delaware River, was authorized by Governor Franklin Delano Roosevelt in 1932. Also known as the Upper Delaware Scenic Byway, Route 97 is not only one of the East Coast's most thrilling and breathtaking highways, but it is also a passageway to the river's plethora of recreational opportunities and the region's rich legacy as New York's first frontier.

As you travel through Port Jervis, you'll be on another notable road. U.S. Route 6, sometimes called "Main Street, U.S.A.," stretches from Provincetown—at the tip of Cape Cod—to Bishop, California. Located at the confluence of the Neversink and Delaware Rivers, and also at the junction of three states (New York, New Jersey, and Pennsylvania), the small city of Port Jervis has been a transportation center for centuries.

23

East
Windham

Prattsville

Windham

9

23

8

Kinderhook

9

Chatham

9W

MARTIN VAN
BUREN NHS

MASSACHUSETTS

30

23A

KAATERSKILL
FALLS

Catskill

Hudson

9H

Claverack

HUNTER
MOUNTAIN

Tannersville

Haines
Falls

OLANA

9

23

CATSKILL PARK

9G

Saugerties

Clermont

82

CLERMONT
SHS

Annandale-on-Hudson

7

STISSING
MOUNTAIN

199

Hancock

17

97

River Rd.

Rhinebeck

Pine
Plains

Kingston

9W

Stanfordville

82

Amenia

PENNSYLVANIA

55

Staatsburg

44

Delaware R.

52

Ellenville

Accord

209

6

New
Paltz

F.D.R.
HOME
N.H.S.

Hyde Park

VANDERBILT
MANSION
N.H.S.

Wassaic

343

Millbrook

INNISFREE
GARDENS

Dover
Plains

Mohonk
Lake

44

87

MINNEWASKA
STATE PARK
RESERVE

ELEANOR
ROOSEVELT
N.H.S.

55

SAM'S
POINT

208

9

CONNECTICUT

17

Pine Bush

22

Narrowsburg

Walden

52

Minisink
Ford

Barryville

84

97

209

Sparrowbush

Port Jervis

5

17

NEW JERSEY

87

The twisting section of Route 97 known as the Hawk's Nest has served as a backdrop for many automotive print and television ads.

The Upper Delaware, which defines New York's border with Pennsylvania, is part of the National Wild and Scenic Rivers System.

Roebling's Delaware Aqueduct, a National Civil Engineering Landmark, originally carried coal-loaded canal boats across the Delaware River.

Originating as a frontier outpost, the city was a stop on the Old Mine Road, America's first one-hundred-mile road. It was also a port on the Delaware & Hudson (D&H) Canal; and thanks to the canal's chief engineer, John B. Jervis, it became an important nineteenth-century railroad hub. When Jervis was hired as a consulting engineer on the Erie Railroad project, he recommended a southerly route through his namesake city. In 1851, the first passenger train steamed through Port Jervis with President Millard Fillmore and Senator Daniel Webster aboard. A brief detour onto Pike Street will allow you to see a relic of the railroad era: the Port Jervis Erie Turntable. Although it is seldom used, it is the largest operating locomotive turntable in America. Built before 1872 and enlarged in the 1930s, it was formerly protected by a roundhouse, which was destroyed by fire in 1987.

The famous Hawk's Nest section of Route 97, which begins in Sparrowbush, is unmatched for white-knuckle driving excitement, revealing surreal scenes as it twists and slithers along a narrow ledge between a granite cliff and a protective stone wall. Watch for an overlook on the left, where you can pull off and enjoy Delaware River views. Starting in the spring, anglers pluck shad, brown and rainbow trout, smallmouth bass, walleye, and American eels from these pure waters. In the summer, roadside outfitters entice travelers to trade their wheels for a raft, tube, or canoe. The river's Class I and II rapids, interspersed with pools and eddies, are novice- and family-friendly. From mid December through early March, the Upper Delaware watershed attracts the largest population of wintering bald eagles in the Northeast. More than one hundred majestic birds annually take advantage of the area's tall trees, clear water, and abundant food supply. Just north of Barryville, you'll see one of the Eagle Institute's bald eagle observation sites, where a sign explains: "The key to successful viewing is patience."

While eagles find these environs hospitable, the first English and Dutch settlers who arrived in the Neversink and Delaware valleys in the last decade of the seventeenth century found themselves in constant peril, due to the wild animals and native peoples inhabiting this harsh wilderness. This was still a frontier outpost at the time of the Battle of Minisink, one of the bloodiest skirmishes of the American Revolution. At Minisink Battleground Park in Minisink Ford, an interpretive trail leads to key sites of the July 22, 1779, engagement. Seeking to exact vengeance for a savage attack on the settlement near what is now Port Jervis, a hastily assembled band of militiamen from New York and New Jersey set out in pursuit of the Iroquois and Tory raiders, who were led by Joseph Brant—a Dartmouth-educated Mohawk warrior who served as a British army colonel. Plans to ambush the enemy were spoiled by a scout's premature firearm discharge, which alerted Brant to the militia's presence. Nearly fifty of these frontier patriots fell during the ensuing battle; their bones lay in this remote place for forty-three years before they were retrieved and properly buried in Goshen.

Development in the region was jumpstarted with the completion of the D&H Canal in 1828. This 108-mile, 108-lock system was built to transport anthracite coal mined in Pennsylvania to the deepwater Hudson River port in Kingston. The D&H Canal was America's first million-dollar private enterprise, and the mule-pulled boats that traveled this route carried millions of tons of coal bound for the New York and New England markets. Abandoned in 1898 due to the advent of more economical rail transportation, many sections of the towpath are now recreational trails, and many vestiges of the canal system remain.

The most notable is Roebling's Delaware Aqueduct, the nation's oldest wire-cable suspension bridge. Built in 1848 and designed by German engineer John A. Roebling (who would later apply similar ideas to the design of the Brooklyn Bridge), this elevated aqueduct for canal boats dramatically cut the time required to cross the Delaware, which was frequently crowded with timber raft traffic. The aqueduct is now a bridge that carries vehicular and pedestrian traffic. You can view historic photos and learn about the advantages of Roebling's design inside the Tollhouse Visitor Contact Station, then walk or drive across the bridge. On the Pennsylvania side, you'll find the Zane Grey Museum, former home of the dentist turned prolific novelist who wrote of fishing adventures on the Delaware before he created a new genre—the western.

Farther north on Route 97, in Narrowsburg, a seasonally operated National Park Service Information Center offers helpful resources, particularly for travelers who want to get out on the river or camp along its banks. During the summer months, you may also want to visit the Fort Delaware Museum of Colonial History. Inside the stockade walls of the reconstructed settlement of Cushetunk, costumed interpreters demonstrate Colonial crafts, such as weaving and blacksmithing, and shed light on the day-to-day lives of those who took on the wilderness. Each January, Narrowsburg's EagleFest celebrates the return of the birds that the Iroquois believed carried messages from the Creator.

Hancock is where Route 97 ends, but it is also where the Delaware River begins at the convergence of its east and west branches. Established in 1806, the town of Hancock is known for its hardwood mills and its quarries, which have supplied bluestone for everything from patios, fireplaces, and sidewalks to the base of the Statue of Liberty. For more than eighty-five years, the Hillerich and Bradsby Company used Hancock timber to make its legendary Louisville Slugger bats swung by such baseball legends as Babe Ruth, Ty Cobb, Joe DiMaggio, and Ted Williams.

From Hancock, the longest free-flowing river in the eastern United States travels 330 miles to its Atlantic Ocean outlet at Delaware Bay. You may not have planned to follow the river back south, but if there's another driver in the car, you may find yourselves on a course back to Port Jervis. This time, just enjoy the ride.

LEFT: *The vertical cliffs of the Mohonk Preserve, the largest privately funded preserve in the state, attract about 50,000 climbers each year to the Shawangunks.*

FACING PAGE: *Looking west from New Paltz, Skytop Tower is an iconic structure in the Shawangunk landscape. It is the fourth in a series of ridgetop towers constructed between 1873 and 1923.*

LEFT: *The carefully preserved and restored fieldstone houses on New Paltz's Huguenot Street offer a glimpse of life in Colonial New York.*

ROUTE 6

Follow New York State Route 299/Main Street west through New Paltz. Turn right on Springtown Road, then left at a fork onto Mountain Rest Road, which becomes Mohonk Road. Turn left on unmarked Clove Road, then left on Towpath Road. After the old Accord train station, turn left onto Granite Road/County Road 27. At the end, turn left and follow U.S. Route 44 and State Route 55 East to the right-hand entrance for Minnewaska State Park Preserve. Leaving Minnewaska, turn left on U.S. 44 and State Route 55 West, then left on U.S. Route 209 South. In Ellenville, turn left and follow State Route 52 East. Take a left in Walden onto State Route 208 North. Turn left and follow U.S. 44 and State Route 55 West to a right on Albany Post Road, heading north. A right on Libertyville Road leads back to New Paltz.

The Nature Conservancy calls the Shawangunks one of earth's "Last Great Places." Located between the Catskill Mountains and the Hudson River, this narrow ridge—a continuation of the Appalachian chain angling from the New Jersey border to Rosendale, New York—is ecologically sensitive and unique. Composed of a base layer of shale capped with concrete-like quartzite conglomerate stone, and fashioned over millions of years by uplift, glacial gouging, and uneven erosion, the Shawangunks' craggy white cliffs provide a diverse habitat for dozens of rare plants and creatures. Fortunately, 25,000 of the 90,000 mountain acres are sheltered within public and private preserves, and grassroots efforts to "Save the Ridge" from development are ongoing. With roughly twelve hundred documented climbing routes, "the Gunks" are a premier destination for rock climbers, but you can also use a tank of gas to scale these pale peaks.

The ridge will loom in the view as you drive west through New Paltz, a progressive university community. Watch for a right turn onto Huguenot Street on the west side of town; this is America's oldest street, where you'll see several well-preserved stone homes built before 1720 and the cemetery where many of New Paltz's founders rest. In 1677, the Esopus Indians sold 40,000 acres along the Wallkill River to twelve Huguenot settlers. The Huguenots were religious and political refugees from France who arrived in America after a temporary stay in die Pfalz, a region along Germany's Rhine River. The Huguenot Historical Society was formed in 1890 to preserve and restore the Colonial edifices and some neighboring homes from subsequent architectural periods. It offers in-depth tours from May through October, but you're welcome to explore this National Historic Landmark District on your own at any time of the year.

Return to Route 299, cross the Wallkill, and make your next right onto Springtown Road to begin your ascent into the Shawangunks. You'll see signs for Mohonk; the native name meaning "lake in the sky" was given both to the famed nineteenth-century Mohonk Mountain House resort and to the adjacent 6,500-acre preserve. Twins Albert and Alfred Smiley purchased 280 acres and a ten-room inn overlooking the reflective waters of Lake Mohonk in 1869. The sprawling, seven-story, turreted Victorian cliff-top castle they built is one of the few remaining grand resorts from that era. Still operated by the Smiley family, the Mohonk Mountain House is a place where guests enjoy tea each afternoon and jackets are required at dinner. Twenty-first-century additions, including a spa and an ice skating pavilion, have been carefully designed to blend with the historic and rustic environs.

The Smiley brothers purchased hundreds of additional parcels in the Shawangunks, and in 1963, their heirs created Mohonk Preserve, forever protecting the rocky cliffs, hemlock ravines, fields, ponds, and streams cherished for centuries by visitors to this mountain hideaway. The gatehouse for

Mohonk Mountain House is on Mountain Rest Road; a day pass entitles you to explore the historic hotel's gardens and grounds, including eighty-five miles of trails and carriage roads for hiking, but you'll only be allowed to enter the Mohonk Mountain House if you've booked lodging or purchased a meal in the dining room. About a mile past the gatehouse, a detour right onto Upper 27 Knolls Road leads to the Mohonk Preserve's Spring Farm Trailhead. Follow the trail a short distance to the top of a rise to enjoy a "Million Dollar View" of the Catskills.

The grand Mohonk Mountain House resort overlooks Lake Mohonk.

You'll drive through preserve lands as you proceed to the next left on Clove Road, and you'll have views of the Rondout Creek as you follow Towpath Road to Accord. Here, a New York, Ontario & Western Railway Company antique caboose stands in front of the 1902 train station. When you reach Routes 44 and 55 and turn east, you'll be in for an ear-popping, uphill drive to the entrance for Minnewaska State Park Preserve. This 12,000-acre tract adjoining Mohonk Preserve is known for its rugged terrain, which challenges those skilled at technical rock climbing, rigorous hiking, and horseback riding. The less adventurous can bike or walk along carriage roads, or you can swim in Lake Minnewaska. Pink and white mountain laurel blooms carpet the forest floor in early summer, and fall's rusty oranges, shocking yellows, and crisp reds give the landscape a lustrous glow.

Originally an Indian path and later known as the Old Mine Road, U.S. Route 209 has been a commercial avenue for centuries. The stretch of U.S. 209 as you head south to Ellenville is named for Clayton "Peg Leg" Bates, the legendary dancer who continued to tap after he lost his left leg in a cotton gin accident at the age of twelve. In 1951, he and his wife converted their sixty-acre turkey farm in the Catskills into the region's first resort for African-Americans.

Between Ellenville and Walden, several detours off Route 52 are worth considering. Turn left on Cragsmoor Road, then continue straight onto Henry Road, and you'll eventually see Stone Church, a picturesque 1897 Episcopalian house of worship in a peaceful, mountain-view setting. Backtrack on Henry Road and turn left on South Gully Road, then right on Sam's Point Road, and you'll reach the Conservation Center at The Nature Conservancy's Sam's Point Preserve. This spot is of extraordinary ecological importance, as it is home to nearly forty rare plant and animal species and the larger of only two ridge-top dwarf pine barrens in the world. The 1.3-mile Ice

A stone arch behind Stone Church in Cragsmoor frames fabulous views of the Shawangunks and Catskills.

One of the most fragile and unique environments in the Shawangunks is protected within The Nature Conservancy's 4,600-acre Sam's Point Preserve.

Lovingly maintained horse farms line Route 199 in eastern Dutchess County, near the Connecticut border.

Caves Trail takes you up among these stunted trees and to the entrance of the caves—the result of deep fissures in the conglomerate bedrock and a jumbled mass of fallen rock debris. The trail, once paved when the caves were a commercial attraction, is now warped and heavily rutted, and the caves remain icy well into the summer months, so proceed cautiously.

In Pine Bush, turn left off Route 52 onto Maple Avenue, then left on Hardenburg Road, to visit Baldwin Vineyards. With its 1786 stone house and neat rows of grapes, Baldwin is the most photogenic of the nine wineries on the Shawangunk Wine Trail. Be sure to sample its highly acclaimed strawberry wine; three-and-a-half pounds of fresh berries go into each bottle. As you meander back toward New Paltz, you'll encounter another wine trail member on Albany Post Road. When you learn that you can sample more than seventy-five of the best New York–made wines at the Rivendell Winery's Vintage New York tasting room, you'll be glad you climbed the Shawangunks in your car and preserved your arm muscles for toasting.

EASTERN DUTCHESS COUNTY
HORSE COUNTRY

ROUTE 7

From Pine Plains, follow New York State Route 199 East to a right in Pulvers Corners on Bean River Road/County Road 59. At the end, turn left on Amenia Pine Plains Road/County Road 83. After Smithfield, watch for a left turn uphill on Flint Hill Road. Turn right onto Cascade Mountain Road, then right on U.S. Route 44 and State Route 22 West. In Amenia, proceed straight onto Routes 22 and 343 West. Turn left on Amenia Wassaic Road/County Road 81. At the end, turn left onto Routes 22 and 343 West. Stay on Route 343 West to Millbrook. Proceed straight onto U.S. 44 West. Turn left on Tyrell Road to visit Innisfree Garden. Backtrack on U.S. 44 East, then take a left on State Route 44A. Turn left on Valley Farm Road, right on Shunpike/County Road 57, then left on Wing Road to reach Millbrook Vineyards and Winery. Return to County Road 57 and head west to a right on State Route 82 North.

Created in 1683, Dutchess was one of New York's original counties. Agricultural tradition runs deep in these gentle hills bounded by the Hudson River to the west and Connecticut to the east. In the nineteenth century, dairying was so prominent that one eastern Dutchess town was known as the "Milky Way." As mechanization revolutionized the industry, however, small dairy farms could not compete, and farmland was sold for development in many areas of the county. Still, eastern Dutchess remains charmingly rural thanks to a new generation of well-heeled farmers who raise grapes and horses in this idyllic setting.

The Hudson Valley region is home to more than thirty thousand horses. As you set out from Pine Plains, you'll know immediately that you're in horse country as you motor past impeccably maintained farms, where Arabians gallop and thoroughbreds graze behind fences that always appear just graced with a fresh coat of white paint.

Stissing House, a tavern and inn in the center of Pine Plains, has welcomed guests since 1782, when Route 199 was the old Salisbury Turnpike—a stagecoach road linking Connecticut and the Hudson River. The hamlet of Hammertown was named for the noise generated by its late eighteenth century scythe factory on the Shekomeko Creek. Here, you'll find one of the area's oldest homes, the circa 1770 red saltbox Harris/Husted House. It is headquarters of the Little Nine Partners Historical Society; this region was part of the 1706 Little Nine Partners Patent, the last of eleven land grants made in Dutchess County.

Along your backroads course to Amenia, you'll pass through the tiny hamlet of Smithfield on County Road 83. Of note is the 1847 Greek Revival Smithfield Church, the third church built on this site since 1750. At the height of the Great Awakening in the middle of the eighteenth century, America's best-known preacher, Methodist evangelist George Whitefield, delivered one of his "fire and brimstone" sermons to a congregation of hundreds from a mighty oak tree that stood in the church's burial ground.

Continue on County Road 83 to a left on Flint Hill Road, a dirt alley that ends at Cascade Mountain Road. Before turning right toward Amenia, you may want to jog left to the entrance for Cascade Mountain Winery, where you can sample the blended wines created by one of the first wineries east of the Hudson.

Amenia—from the Latin *amoena*, or "pleasant to the eye"—was named by an early settler, Dr. Thomas Young, who is also credited with naming the state of Vermont. On Amenia Wassaic Road, you'll pass the site where Gail Borden Jr. opened America's first plant for condensing, pasteurizing, and bottling milk in 1853, a development that fueled the local dairy industry. When you return to Routes 22 and 343 West, you'll drive alongside Wassaic State Forest, a 488-acre reclaimed woodland. As you approach Millbrook on Route 343, watch for another landmark on the right: the Nine Partners Meeting House, built in 1780 by Quaker settlers from Cape Cod, Nantucket, and Rhode Island.

Millbrook is an epicenter of equestrian activity, where horse trials are held each summer and the Millbrook Hunt is a fall tradition. A right turn at the junction of State Route 343 and U.S. Route 44 leads to the quaint village center, but if you proceed straight onto U.S. 44 West, you'll discover some of Millbrook's most intriguing attractions, including remarkable gardens, a world-class winery, and a castle. From May through mid October, Innisfree Garden blossoms much as Walter Beck envisioned in 1930. After he and his wife, Marion, bequeathed their 150-acre garden surrounding a 40-acre glacial lake for the public's enjoyment in 1960, landscape architect Lester Collins expanded on Beck's original design.

On State Route 44A, stop at the Mary Flagler Cary Arboretum, home to the Institute of Ecosystem Studies, one of the largest ecology research and education centers in the world. While much of the 2,000-acre tract donated by Cary, heiress to the Standard Oil fortune, is reserved for research, the public is welcome to explore four nature trails, a fern glen, and a perennial garden from mid April through October. The Millbrook Vineyards and Winery is your next stop, and while you may not have heard of owner John Dyson, you'll recognize in a heartbeat the enduring slogan he championed as state commerce commissioner in the mid 1970s: "I Love New York." Since 1981, Dyson and his wife, who also own wineries in California, have earned high praises for their vinifera wines, and you can sample them year-round following a tour of the wine-making process.

On a hill above the picturesque vineyard, you'll notice a fortress-like structure. Wing's Castle was constructed from salvaged materials by artist Peter Wing and his wife, Toni Ann, over more than two decades. Tours of this rather eccentric home are offered seasonally—at least until the Wings get their asking price of $5.85 million.

ABOVE: *Amenia, settled in 1704, was known as the "Milky Way" in the mid nineteenth century due to its proliferation of dairy farms.*

RIGHT: *The Oriental-inspired landscape of Millbrook's Innisfree Garden utilizes native plants and locally gathered stones in intimate planted niches.*

The Clermont State Historic Site is one of several lavish estates owned by leading New Yorkers in the Mid-Hudson Valley. Clermont was home to seven generations of one branch of the Livingston family from 1728 until 1962.

The red brick Saugerties Lighthouse, built in 1869 to replace the original 1838 light, is visible from Clermont's west lawn. Extensively restored, it is accessible via a footpath on the Hudson's western shore. It is open for both tours and overnight lodging.

You can follow Route 82 North straight back to Pine Plains, but there are several detours to consider. North of Stanfordville, a left on Stissing Lane leads to Buttercup Farm Sanctuary, a 500-acre Audubon center with six miles of hiking trails through diverse terrain. As many as eighty bird species have been observed here on peak May days. Farther north on Route 82, you'll spy the Attlebury Schoolhouse, a restored, nineteenth-century one-room school. A walk or a picnic on the grounds affords views of 1,403-foot Stissing Mountain, the area's tallest peak.

Just before you reach Pine Plains, turn left on Lake Road, where you'll find The Nature Conservancy's Thompson Pond Nature Preserve, a National Natural Landmark. Nearly fifteen thousand years ago, the Thompson Pond Basin was formed as a melting ice mass created a depression or "kettle." Over time, this large water body at the base of Stissing Mountain has been divided into three interconnected lakes. The 507-acre preserve, with its calcareous wetlands and upland forests, is a popular hiking and birding destination and an abundant habitat for nearly 400 plant species and more than 150 types of birds. If you're feeling energetic, hike the steep trail to the restored 1934 fire tower atop Stissing Mountain. From this perch high above horse country, you'll be able to appreciate fully just how green and serene much of Dutchess County remains.

KINDERHOOK TO HYDE PARK
A PRESIDENTIAL PATH

ROUTE 8

From Kinderhook, follow New York State Route 9H South. In Claverack, continue south on this route when it joins State Route 23. Proceed straight onto U.S. Route 9 South, then turn right in Clermont onto County Road 6. After visiting Clermont Historic Site, backtrack on County Road 6 to a right on State Route 9G South. Turn right onto Annandale Road in Annandale-on-Hudson, then bear left onto River Road/County Road 103. Watch for a left turn onto Rhinecliff Road. In the center of Rhinebeck, turn right on U.S. 9 South. Take the first right onto Mill Road/County Road 85 to visit Wilderstein. Return briefly to U.S. 9 South, then turn right and follow Old Post Road through Staatsburg, and back to U.S. 9 South to Hyde Park.

The Mid-Hudson Valley has been home to an extraordinary number of influential Americans. Some were heirs to the rich property holdings granted by their ancestors. A few rose to great heights in spite of humble origins. And others, wooed by views of rippling water and purple mountains, built grand riverside mansions with fortunes made elsewhere. All left behind a remarkable legacy, not only of magnificent estates now accessible to all, but also of ideas and actions that influenced the course of history.

Just fifty miles separate Kinderhook in Columbia County and Hyde Park in Dutchess County, but in this short span, you'll cross paths with presidents and many other influential New Yorkers. Begin your day in rural Kinderhook, where Abraham and Maria Van Buren, Dutch farmers and tavern keepers, welcomed a son in 1782 who would become the first president born in the United States. Martin Van Buren was the original career politician, serving as state senator, U.S. senator, New York governor, secretary of state, and then vice president under Andrew Jackson before being elected to a single presidential term in 1836. At the Martin Van Buren National Historic Site in Kinderhook, visitors can tour Lindenwald, the architecturally intriguing and artifact-filled retirement home of the eighth president—a man of many nicknames including "the Little Magician," "the Red Fox of Kinderhook," and "Old Kinderhook," or just "OK." Historians have largely judged Van Buren, who inherited a nation in economic crisis, to have been just OK as a president, but he played a key role in the development of an Independent Treasury and America's political party system.

Clermont State Historic Site, the next estate to visit, provides a glimpse into the life of a prominent New York family over the course of two centuries. The first Robert Livingston, a Scotsman, arrived in New York shortly after England had seized the colony from the Dutch. He quickly forged ties to both the English rulers and the local Dutch aristocracy, and in 1686, he was granted a 160,000-acre manor. Robert Livingston Jr. built Clermont on his 13,000 inherited acres, and his son, Robert R. Livingston, expanded the family's holdings by marrying Margaret Beekman.

When Clermont was burned in 1777 by British troops, Margaret oversaw its reconstruction in time to welcome General and Mrs. George Washington in 1782. Margaret and Robert's son, Chancellor Robert R. Livingston, was the estate's most notable owner. He helped draft the Declaration of Independence, served as the first U.S. minister of foreign affairs, administered the oath of office to Washington, negotiated the Louisiana Purchase, and collaborated with Robert Fulton on development of the steamboat. Genealogical charts in the visitors' center at Clermont will help you sort out all the Roberts.

On Route 9G, you'll pass the entrance to Bard College in the tiny hamlet of Annandale-on-Hudson. Founded as St. Stephen's College in 1860, the liberal arts school is situated on five hundred riverfront acres. Although graduates Walter Becker and Donald Fagen of Steely Dan vowed in the song "My Old School" that they'd never return, many visitors flock here, particularly for the Bard Music Festival, held each summer at the Frank Gehry–designed Richard B. Fisher Center for the Performing Arts.

Montgomery Place, located adjacent to Bard College, is a 434-acre River Road estate first owned by Chancellor Robert R. Livingston's sister, Janet, the widow of Revolutionary War hero Richard Montgomery. Like Clermont, Montgomery Place was held by family members—including Janet's brother Edward, secretary of state to Andrew Jackson—until the late twentieth century. The mansion showcases many periods of ownership, and the landscape reflects the nineteenth-century touch of noted designer Andrew Jackson Downing.

Another picturesque landscape awaits at Poet's Walk Park. From the parking area just off River Road, you can explore two miles of trails through the former Rokeby Estate, home at times to Livingstons, Delanos, and even William Astor, the richest man in America. German gardener Hans Jacob Ehlers designed the Poet's Walk in 1849 in honor of Washington Irving and Fitz-Green Halleck, who were reputedly inspired by the property's Hudson River overlooks.

From River Road, turn east toward the center of Rhinebeck, a cosmopolitan village oft-equated to Long Island's chi-chi Hamptons. At the junction with U.S. Route 9, you'll see the venerable Beekman Arms, America's

Thanks to the conservation efforts of Scenic Hudson, a nonprofit land trust and environmental organization, Poet's Walk Park remains a magnificent setting for quiet contemplation and artistic inspiration.

ABOVE: *The metallic and curvaceous Richard B. Fisher Center for the Performing Arts at Bard College is the only performance venue on the East Coast designed by internationally renowned architect Frank Gehry.*

RIGHT: *Stunning views of the Hudson River are just one of the enticements of the Vanderbilt Mansion National Historic Site; the grounds of the Gilded Age estate are open free to visitors daily from dawn until dusk.*

oldest continuously operated hotel. George Washington, Benedict Arnold, and Alexander Hamilton all slept, ate, and drank here; Benjamin Harrison was at "the Beek" in 1888 when he learned he'd been nominated for president; and Franklin Roosevelt spoke from the inn's front porch at the conclusion of each of his gubernatorial and presidential campaigns.

You'll hear more about F.D.R. at Wilderstein, the multigabled, Queen Anne-style Victorian mansion on Morton Road. The estate, with its Joseph Burr Tiffany interiors and landscape by Calvert Vaux, was owned by the Suckley family from 1852 until 1991, when its final and most notable resident died at the age of ninety-nine. Margaret Suckley, called "Daisy" by Roosevelt, her distant cousin, was the president's frequent companion, confidante, and likely lover. Daisy gave F.D.R. his beloved Scottie, Fala; he shared with her details of such weighty matters as the planned D-day invasion.

U.S. 9, which eventually becomes Manhattan's Broadway, roughly follows the path of the old Albany to New York Post Road. When you reach the hamlet of Staatsburg, veer off U.S. 9 onto Old Post Road to visit Staatsburgh State Historic Site. The sixty-five-room Gilded Age mansion

A PLACE OF HER OWN

In 1921, Franklin Delano Roosevelt's political ambitions were suddenly threatened when a near-fatal case of polio left him paralyzed from the waist down. His political advisor, Louis Howe, turned to Anna Eleanor Roosevelt, the distant cousin that Franklin had married in 1905, to keep Roosevelt's name and ideas in front of the Democratic party. Exceedingly shy, rather awkward at nearly six feet tall, perpetually pregnant during the first decade of their marriage, and meekly tolerant of the meddlesome omnipresence of Franklin's doting mother, Sara Delano Roosevelt, Eleanor found she had a knack for speech-making and political maneuvering. She and Franklin, in spite of their marital transgressions and personal heartaches, were a formidable political duo. Eleanor went where FDR could not, traveling the nation during the Great Depression to bring back stories of the plight of the poor and crisscrossing the globe to visit American troops during World War II.

After Franklin's death in 1945, Eleanor continued to travel extensively, as well as write, speak, and advocate for humanitarian causes. As chair of the United Nations Commission on Human Rights, she oversaw the adoption in 1948 of the Universal Declaration of Human Rights. President Roosevelt's successor, Harry Truman,

dubbed her the "First Lady of the World," and in 1960, John F. Kennedy visited Eleanor at her home in Hyde Park to seek her blessing for his presidential campaign.

The Democratic Party's matriarch lived out the final decades of her life at Val-Kill Cottage, the modest home that was her sanctuary from the tumult of her public and private life. In 1924, while picnicking alongside Fall Kill stream on the Roosevelts' Hyde Park estate, Eleanor lamented that her mother-in-law would soon close the big house for the season. Franklin suggested that she and her female political friends build a year-round cottage on the estate. Stone Cottage was completed a year later. A second building, which housed the experimental furnishings manufacturer Val-Kill Industries from 1926 until 1936, was reconfigured into apartments for Eleanor and her secretary. Both are now preserved at the Eleanor Roosevelt National Historic Site, the only National Historic Site dedicated to a First Lady. Visitors to this peaceful retreat, located two miles from the "big house" on Route 9G in Hyde Park, will be struck by how humbly this influential woman—who welcomed everyone from great-grandchildren to emperors at her Hyde Park hideaway—lived until her death in 1962 at the age of seventy-eight.

was designed in beaux-arts style by the prestigious firm of McKim, Mead, and White for Ruth Livingston and Ogden Mills. Ruth's great-grandfather, Morgan Lewis, was the third governor of New York, and he purchased the riverfront estate in 1792; Ogden's father made a bundle in banking and railroads during the California Gold Rush. Ruth and Ogden occupied this stately mansion for only two fall months each year. A riverside hiking trail links Mills Mansion with the marina, campground, and environmental center at Margaret Lewis Norrie State Park.

Continuing south on U.S. 9 to Hyde Park, you'll soon see the imposing gates of Vanderbilt Mansion, another McKim, Mead, and White master-piece. The fifty-four-room abode, with its Italian-style terraced garden and spectacular river vistas, was a mere "cottage" to Louise and Frederick Vanderbilt. Frederick was the most private of the eight grandchildren of shipping and railroad baron Commodore Cornelius Vanderbilt, and the only one to increase his inherited wealth, from $10 million to more than $70 million by the time of his death in 1938. Tours allow visitors to see the Vanderbilts' impressive collection of art and furnishings, which cost them twice the amount of the mansion.

The 211-acre Vanderbilt estate and the nearby home of Franklin Delano Roosevelt are operated jointly by the National Park Service. FDR's Springwood is modest in comparison to the Mills and Vanderbilt mansions, but the New York governor and U.S. president's Hyde Park home is steeped in mystique. From films and exhibits in the Henry A. Wallace Visitor and Education Center, to personal effects ranging from the president's bassinet to his hand-operated 1936 Ford Phaeton in the Presidential Library and Museum, visitors can fully immerse themselves in the life and times of America's thirty-second and longest-serving president.

Unlike Van Buren, who rose from humble origins to lead the nation, Roosevelt was a member of the Hudson Valley's landed elite. Nevertheless, he came to sympathize with the plight of poor Americans and took radical action to alleviate their suffering with his bold and innovative New Deal initiatives. As you walk the grounds he cherished, view his boyhood bird collection, listen to the comforting words he uttered at some of the nation's tensest moments, stand quietly in the rose garden where he is buried beside his wife and polit-ical partner, Eleanor, and ponder the physical limitations that kept him confined to the wheelchair that still sits in his study, you'll come to know a man whose influence still reverberates far beyond his home on the Hudson.

THE CATSKILLS
IMMORTAL MOUNTAINS

"Welcome to the land of Rip Van Winkle," reads a sign that greets motorists headed west on Route 23 toward the looming mountain skyline. It was in these ancient, gray sandstone peaks, of course, that Washington Irving's likable character observed strange beings playing at ninepins,

ROUTE 9

From Catskill, follow New York State Route 23 West to Prattsville. Backtrack on Route 23 East to State Route 23A East through the Catskill Park. When Route 23A East ends, follow U.S. Route 9W North to Route 23 East. Proceed across the Rip Van Winkle Bridge (toll), then turn right on State Route 9G South to the left-hand entrance for Olana State Historic Site.

The Catskills are replete with inspiring mountain vistas, such as this view of North-South Lake in Catskill Park.

Tucked among the tall pines, St. John the Baptist Ukrainian Catholic Church in Hunter was built in the traditional timber blockwork style common to the Ukrainian highlands.

The 175-foot upper falls is only half the spectacle you'll behold when you reach Kaaterskill Falls at the end of a moderate, half-mile hike.

LEFT: *The still pools, dense hemlock stands, and sculptural rocks found along Kaaterskill Creek appear much as they did when Thomas Cole committed them to canvas in the nineteenth century.*

BELOW: *The Rip Van Winkle Bridge has carried travelers into the heart of the legendary Catskill Mountains, where its fictional namesake slumbered for two decades, since it opened to traffic in 1935.*

Pratt Rocks are a unique Catskills attraction.

quaffed their liquor, and then slept for a night that lasted twenty years. Storytellers and artists elevated these misty hills sheathed in boreal forests to mythological status long before the region became an accessible and popular vacationland. The legendary scenes captured on canvas and recorded in fables spring to life as you follow the curvy path of this skyward drive.

In East Windham, be sure to pull off Route 23 at Point Lookout. On clear days, this overlook beside the dramatically situated Point Lookout Mountain Inn affords views of five states. As Route 23 continues to climb, you'll enter the Catskill Park, a 700,000-acre area (almost as large as Rhode Island) composed of private and public lands in four counties. Since the park was created in 1885, the state's holdings, protected within the Catskill Forest Preserve, have expanded from 34,000 to nearly 300,000 acres. With ninety-eight peaks surpassing three thousand feet, the Catskills are one of New York's most popular winter destinations; Windham, home to the Windham Mountain ski area, is the first of several cheery ski towns you'll encounter.

As you approach Prattsville, you'll see Pratt Rocks, one of the state's quirkiest attractions. Zadock Pratt, who came to the Catskills as a small boy, labored and scrimped until he could afford to open a tannery on the Schoharie Creek, taking advantage of the abundance of hemlock bark, essential to the leather-making process. Within twenty years, he'd amassed a fortune, built an entire town, opened a bank where he minted his own money, and won a seat in Congress. According to local lore, when a panhandling stonecutter wandered through in 1843, Pratt gave him fifty cents to carve his profile on a mountain ledge. Pleased with the result, he commissioned his entire life story chiseled into the cliff face. Visitors who climb the serpentine inclines at Pratt Rocks will see a horse, a hemlock, and other symbols, including Pratt's coat of arms and motto: "Do Well and Doubt Not." What began as a monument to vanity became a memorial to Pratt's only son, George, a Civil War colonel, whose bust was added to the five-hundred-foot rock wall after he died at the Battle of Manassas. Without an heir to his empire, Pratt isn't remembered far beyond the boundaries of the town he transformed, but in Prattsville, where his 1829 home is now the Zadock Pratt Museum, he remains a legend.

You'll pass public fishing areas as you follow Route 23A East along the trout-filled Schoharie Creek toward Hunter and Tannersville, two charming mountain towns that bustle with visitors during the winter ski, spring fly-fishing, summer festival, and fall leaf-peeping seasons at Hunter

Mountain. The eye-catching, cedar log complex you'll see on the left before you reach Hunter is St. John the Baptist Ukrainian Catholic Church. The 1962 basilica and other structures were built without nails, in traditional Ukrainian architectural style. Visitors can sample Ukrainian cuisine at the congregation's summer Sunday brunches.

As Route 23A descends into Haines Falls, watch for a left onto North Lake Road/County Road 18, where you'll find the entrance to North-South Lake—a state beach, campground, and preserve. Hikers who follow the Escarpment Trail to landmark points like Artist's Rock and the site of the once-grand Catskill Mountain House—which counted three presidents among its elite guests between 1824 and 1941—will enjoy views committed to canvas by Hudson River School painters including Thomas Cole, father of this first American school of landscape painting.

Kaaterskill Falls, New York's highest two-tiered waterfall and another oft-painted scene, can be reached via a trail that diverges from the Escarpment Trail, or you can continue 1.3 miles past North Lake Road on Route 23A to a right-hand-side parking area. Exercise caution when you make your way along the road's slender shoulder to smaller Bastion Falls, located at the trailhead for the rocky and rooty, moderate half-mile climb to Kaaterskill Falls. The 260-foot double cascade is at its most awe-inspiring in the spring, when melting snow and ice increase the rush of water spilling over rocky ledges.

Route 23A takes some exhilarating S-turns as you continue your descent toward Catskill. Before you follow Route 23 East across the Rip Van Winkle Bridge, turn left onto Spring Street/Route 385. Tours of Cedar Grove, Cole's home and studio, offer insight into the remarkable career of this largely self-taught Englishman, whose first depictions of the Catskills, painted in 1825, took the New York City art world by storm. More than seventy other artists would follow Cole's lead, creating luminous and highly detailed paintings that engendered reverence for the beauty of uniquely American scenes.

After you cross to the east bank of the Hudson, visit the home of Frederic Edwin Church, Cole's student and one of the school's most accomplished painters. Known for his colossal canvases, Church's largest work was Olana, the estate he created with the help of designer Calvert Vaux. Influenced by the Moorish architecture he'd seen in the Middle East, Church fashioned a home rich in texture and color, and he constructed and expanded it between 1870 and 1890. He also devoted considerable energy to designing the property's roads so that spectacular scenes of the Hudson and Catskills were calculatingly revealed.

As you savor these vistas, blissfully little altered by the passage of time, you'll realize that even if old Rip had slumbered for one hundred years, he still would have descended from the mountains, stroking his beard in bewilderment, yet secure in the knowledge that "there stood the Kaatskill Mountains—there ran the silver Hudson."

PART III

AROUND ALBANY
A NURTURING ENVIRONMENT

ABOVE:
Mine Kill State Park in North Blenheim offers a variety of outdoor pleasures, including picnicking alongside Mine Kill Falls.

FACING PAGE:
With more than 500 farms, agriculture remains the leading industry of Schoharie County in east-central New York, and agritourism is increasingly important to the region.

It wasn't New York's first capital. It's certainly not the state's largest or most glamorous city. Yet Albany is at the hub of a region that has, for centuries, played a key supporting role in the development not only of the state but of the nation—and its national pastime. Set out from this former wilderness outpost on the Hudson, and you'll soon be following in the footsteps of Native American traders, standing on earth that absorbed the blood of determined patriots, marveling at the wonders of natural and engineered waterways, or viewing a bat that was once clutched in the meaty hands of the "Sultan of Swat."

Being first or biggest isn't everything, after all. The American Revolution did not begin nor was it won in central New York, but it is here where a crucial victory ensured the future of the new union. New York City owes its status as the world financial capital to two canals and two rivers that converge near Waterford. And Cooperstown will forever be home to Babe Ruth and other legends of baseball, even if it's not where the game was originally devised.

From growing the grains that fed America's upstart army, to providing water that urban New Yorkers drink today, this bountiful region has nurtured New York's aspirations for freedom, fortune, and fame for centuries. You'll have no doubt after exploring Albany's surroundings that this is the right location for the capital of the Empire State.

THE HELDERBERGS
IF MOUNTAINS COULD TALK,
WHAT SECRETS THEY WOULD TELL

ROUTE 10

From Delmar, follow New York State Route 443 West. Turn right on Orchard Street, then left on Game Farm Road to visit Five Rivers Environmental Education Center. Continue on Game Farm Road to a right on New Scotland South Road. When it ends, turn left and follow State Route 85 South to a right on State Route 157 West. Turn left onto State Route 156 West. In Berne, turn left and return to Delmar via Route 443 East.

Even if you've never set foot in New York State, you've probably heard of the Adirondacks and the Catskills. But what about the Helderbergs? New York's third mountain chain may lack name recognition, but this jagged ridge west of Albany is rife with wild beauty and historic intrigue. The region's splendor is remarkably accessible today, but for centuries, the Helderbergs held secrets.

Actually, the murky origins of these mountains date to the Paleozoic Era some 250 million to 540 million years ago. As you head west from Delmar, envision a time when this area was submerged beneath the shallow Utica Sea, its waters teeming with tiny shelled creatures. Layers of sedimentary rock were formed as each generation of marine organisms deposited its shells upon the seafloor. When the earth shifted and lifted, the waters receded, exposing the cave-riddled limestone cliffs of the Helderberg escarpment.

Fossilized evidence of ancient sea life is apparent when you get up close to the cliffs, but before you begin your ascent into the mountains, stop at Five Rivers Environmental Education Center on Game Farm Road to learn about Albany County's extant wildlife. This 400-acre nature preserve is located on the site of New York's first and only State Experimental Game Farm, created between 1933 and 1936 by a resident company of the Civilian Conservation Corps. For nearly forty years, the game farm's researchers revolutionized wildlife management practices,

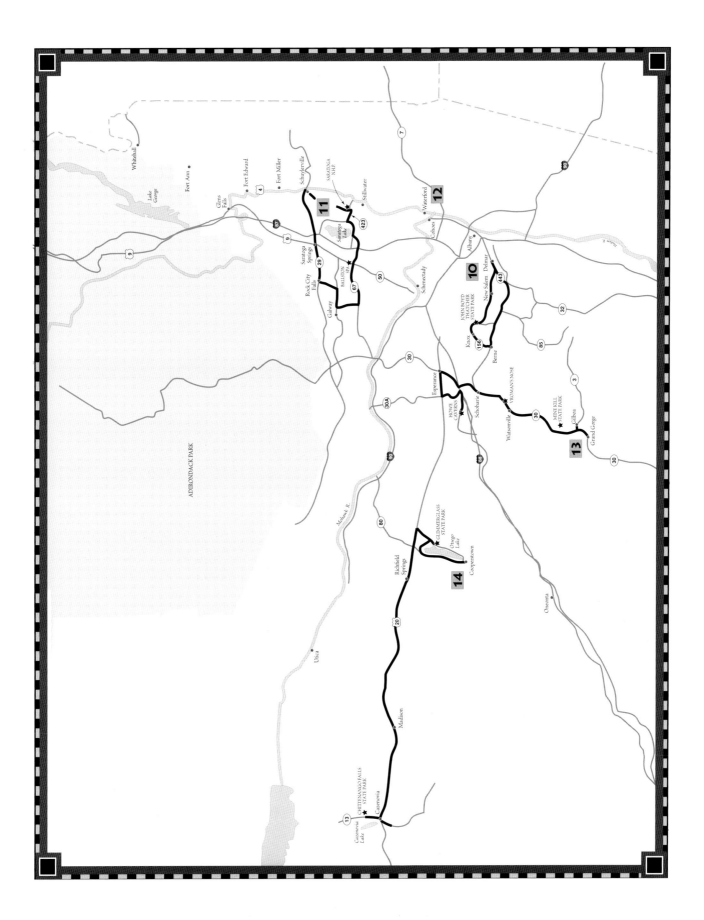

Autumn carpets the Helderberg escarpment in rich shades of rust, orange, and gold.

LEFT: *A guided tour of the Indian Ladder Trail, when available, offers insight into the Helderbergs' unique geology, but no explanation is necessary to appreciate the wonder of standing on a ledge beneath the silvery shower of Minelot Falls.*

BELOW: *Thompson's Lake—an example of a limestone sinkhole— has no surface outlet; it drains through a cave at its southern end.*

solidifying New York's position at the forefront of the conservation movement. In 1972, Five Rivers became a public facility dedicated to protecting and promoting an appreciation for environmental resources. Visitors can observe butterflies, listen for the chatter of eastern bluebirds or an owl's haunting hoot, and perhaps spy a deer, beaver, or wild turkey along trails that range from a quarter-mile to two miles in length.

The distinctive mountain formation will emerge as you travel through the tranquil towns of New Scotland and New Salem along Route 85. Route 157 will take you atop the Helderberg plateau and into John Boyd Thacher State Park. The park is home to ball fields, playgrounds, picnic areas, and a swimming pool, but exploration, not recreation, is its strongest draw. Near the entrance, watch for the Cliff Edge Overlook on the right. This parking area, open during daylight hours year-round, provides the best views of the calcareous cliffs and the luxuriant Mohawk Valley that you can experience without a hike. You won't, however, want to miss the opportunity to walk beside the cliff face and under a waterfall along the famed Indian Ladder Trail.

Albany, which became New York's capital in 1797, was one of the first permanent settlements in the American colonies. Established in 1624 as Fort Orange, it was a frontier outpost where Dutch traders acquired beaver pelts from Native American trappers. The fur trade must have been lucrative for the Mohawks, who trekked east from the Schoharie Valley across the rugged mountain wilderness, felling trees with hatchets to create the original Indian Ladder. The series of tree-stump footholds that scaled the limestone cliffs was in use until the 1820s, when a road was constructed to replace the path.

Today, the half-mile Indian Ladder Trail, open from May through mid November, is a fairly easy hike. If you have time and stamina, you can follow the two-mile Cliff Top Trail from the parking overlook to the Indian Ladder. However, much easier trail access is found farther west on Route 157, inside the state park's main entrance. Although it is not open to the public, the historical marker for Tory Cave, located near the trailhead, will fuel your imagination. This was the hiding place of Royalist spy Jacob Salsbury during the American Revolutionary War, but it didn't prove secretive enough to prevent his capture.

As you descend steep steps and begin your walk along the cliff-hugging Indian Ladder Trail, examine the rocky wall for fossils and fissures, the characteristic vertical cracks caused by rain erosion. Limestone's solubility is the reason for the prevalence of caves and underground streams in this mountain chain.

Sinkholes are also common to limestone formations; they're formed when underground water causes a surface collapse. Farther west on Route 157, Thompson's Lake State Park is a popular camping and fishing destination made possible by this geologic phenomenon. Turn right onto Ketcham Road, then left on Nature Center Way, to visit the Emma Treadwell Thacher Nature Center, which features hands-on exhibits and a number of trails, including a short and easy path to the lakeshore.

As your drive continues through the hilly farmlands of the towns of Knox and Berne, pause to reflect on the ease with which you crossed the Helderberg ridge. Don't doubt, however, the difficulty this obstacle presented to Native American trailblazers and would-be settlers. The Palatine German refugees who first settled these towns actually came from the Schoharie Valley to the west. While Helderberg is derived from a German phrase meaning "clear mountain," these seventeenth-century squatters were fortunate that the escarpment kept their secret from Kiliaen Van Rensselaer. They lived rent-free on the Dutch lord's lands for nearly fifty years.

SARATOGA
A PIVOTAL PLACE

Visitors flock to Saratoga for the excitement of thoroughbred horseracing and the invigorating effects of effervescent springs. There is, however, another side to Saratoga, one that is best experienced not at a run, gallop, or even a trot, but at a leisurely gait that allows you to ponder pivotal moments in history—such as the American colonists' first significant Revolutionary War victory and the invention of America's favorite snack food.

Start your day at Saratoga National Historical Park in Stillwater, where you'll trod ground upon which the course of world events was altered. Here, in what is considered one of the most decisive military engagements in history, American troops thwarted the offensive of British General John Burgoyne, who endeavored to quell the rebellion by severing communications between the northern and southern colonies. The Revolutionary forces' surprising success at the Battles of Saratoga, which forced Burgoyne's surrender on October 17, 1777, bolstered the Americans' ambitions and spurred France to ally with, and provide critical aid to, the fledgling nation.

The Saratoga battlefield was established as a state park in 1927 and became a national park in 1938. The grounds and visitors' center are open year-round, but if you visit between April and mid November, you can drive the nine-mile Park Tour Road. Allow at least two hours, as there are ten stops that tell the story of the dramatic conflict. Interpretive signs, audio recordings, and (at times) historical re-enactors bring to life the tales of those who perished and those who persevered. Among the historic figures who played a prominent role in these historic events were Polish engineer Thaddeus Kosciuszko, whose design for fortifications was key to the American strategy against Burgoyne, and Benedict Arnold, who took a bullet in the leg while leading a fierce charge against the foe. Had that wound been fatal, Arnold might be revered as one of America's most valiant heroes.

After you leave the battleground, travel briefly on Route 9P along the southern shore of 4,000-acre Saratoga Lake. While the details of the story lack the crispness you'd expect, local lore has it that in 1853, Native American cook George Crum invented the potato chip at a lakeside resort. A patron, it is told, sent his too-thick French fries back to the kitchen. In a

ROUTE 11

From Saratoga National Historical Park, follow New York State Route 32 South to State Route 423 West. Turn left onto State Route 9P South, then left onto County Road 108/Plains Road. Proceed straight onto State Route 67 West. Turn right and follow State Route 50 North to Ballston Spa. In town, turn left on Washington Street, left on Bath Street, right on Front Street, and left on Charlton Street. Turn right and pick up Route 67 West again. Turn right onto County Road 52/Jockey Street, then right on County Road 45/Galway Road and right onto Bliss Road to Johnston's Winery. Return to Galway Road heading east, then turn left on County Road 49/Milton Rock City Road. Turn right and follow New York State Route 29 East to Schuylerville. Turn right onto U.S. Route 4 and State Route 32, then watch for a right on County Road 338/Burgoyne Road to the Saratoga Battle Monument.

RIGHT: *Stops along the Saratoga National Historical Park's nine-mile Park Tour Road include American camp locations, battle sites, and British defensive positions overlooking the Hudson River.*

BELOW: *Saratoga Lake is a popular boating and bass-fishing destination ringed with residences, inns, and restaurants.*

Saratoga Monument in Victory features four arch-shaped niches that house statues of three of the generals who led the victorious American troops in the decisive Revolutionary War battle: Philip Schuyler, Horatio Gates, and Daniel Morgan. The south-facing niche is vacant, an eternal rebuke to Benedict Arnold, the hero turned traitor.

British General John Burgoyne surrenders to Horatio Gates at Saratoga in October 1777. The Granger Collection, New York

pique, the curmudgeonly Crum fried up a batch of paper-thin potatoes, which were unexpectedly well-received. Saratoga chips became the house specialty and were soon packaged and distributed region-wide.

When you reach Ballston Spa—which competed with Saratoga Springs for wealthy nineteenth-century vacationers who came to "take the waters" at natural mineral baths—you'll wind your way past the Washington Street birthplace of another inventor with a much-disputed claim to fame. American Civil War hero Abner Doubleday has been credited, likely erroneously, with devising the game of baseball. On Route 50 in Ballston Spa, you'll also find the National Bottle Museum, which pays homage to America's first industry. By 1850, there were forty glassmaking factories in New York. Millions of bottles were manufactured annually just to meet the demands of those bottling the purportedly healing mineral waters of Saratoga County.

As you head north to connect with Route 29 East, you'll pass through Galway, settled by Scottish immigrants in 1774. At Johnston's Winery, which is open on weekends year-round, you will learn that although this region's climate is not hospitable to grape-growing, intriguing wines can be crafted from heartier fruits, including blueberries, cherries, and peaches.

Route 29 takes a quick jog through downtown Saratoga Springs and passes the New York State Military Museum. Housed in an 1889 armory, the museum holds ten thousand artifacts dating from the Revolution to Operation Desert Storm, including the world's largest collection of American Civil War flags.

In Schuylerville, turn south toward the aptly named village of Victory, where you'll find the Saratoga Monument. Completed in 1883, this 154-foot, 6-inch granite obelisk marks the location of Burgoyne's camp in the final days prior to his bitter defeat and commemorates the turning point in America's struggle for independence.

In season, you can climb the tower's 188 steps to a viewing platform. Ascend slowly and pause to contemplate the sacrifices made by those who risked all to secure Americans' rights to life, liberty, and the pursuit of happiness. After you return to ground level, you'll be free to pursue what-ever Saratoga adventure beckons to you, whether it's soaking in the springs, watching the Racino's video slot wheels spin, or wagering on a long shot.

WATERFORD TO WHITEHALL
FEEDING THE DREAM

Henry Hudson turned his ship, the *Half Moon*, around just south of the great falls, where the Mohawk River pours into the water artery that now bears his name. You'll catch a glimpse of Cohoes Falls, New York's second largest waterfall, as you cross the bridge that connects the towns of Cohoes and Waterford.

The flow of Cohoes Falls is often curtailed due to its modern role in hydroelectric generation, but nothing can diminish the significance of this cascade at the convergence of the mighty Mohawk and Hudson Rivers, New York's natural liquid highway. As you enter Waterford, you'll discover that you are also at the crossroads of America's most important man-made waterway.

The completion of the 60-mile Champlain Canal in 1823 and the 363-mile Erie Canal in 1825 marked the fulfillment of Governor DeWitt Clinton's ambition to "create the greatest inland trade ever witnessed" by linking the Hudson, the St. Lawrence, and the Great Lakes. Doubters labeled the plan "Clinton's Ditch," but the governor prophesied in 1816 that this elaborate system of canals would open the continent's interior and transform Manhattan into "the granary of the world, the emporium of commerce, the seat of manufactures, the focus of great moneyed operations and the concentrating point of vast disposable, and accumulating capital."

Settled by Dutch traders in 1622, Waterford is the country's oldest continuously incorporated village. It became the junction for the two canals following a decision in 1903 to expand the system to accommodate larger barges. Don't leave town without driving along Flight Lock Road, where you can see the Waterford Flight of Locks in action. Completed in 1915, this set of five locks at the entrance to the Erie Canal, built to bypass Cohoes Falls, lifts boats 169 feet. No other system in the world achieves this height differential in such a short span.

Peebles Island State Park, bounded by the Hudson River on the east and by a branch of the Mohawk River to the west, is also worth a visit. Inhabited originally by the Mahicans, the island was a strategic outpost for colonial defenses during the Revolutionary War. The park, accessible from 2nd Street in Waterford, is home to hiking trails, picnic areas, and a visitors' center for the Erie Canalway National Heritage Corridor, which extends west to Buffalo.

Don't heed the call of the west, however. The road less traveled from Waterford heads north along the Erie Canal's lesser known yet equally influential sister canal. Vestiges of the original Champlain Canal are evident in Waterford. As you proceed north on New York State Route 32 and U.S. Route 4, you'll see that the updated Champlain Canal, part of the 524-mile New York State Canal System, is in many places a channel of the Hudson River. Twelve locks between Waterford and Whitehall make this passage navigable. Lock 2 is a particularly scenic place to stop in the hopes of seeing a lock in operation, filling with water to raise a craft headed north or emptying to lower a boat traveling south.

ROUTE 12

From Cohoes, travel north on New York State Route 32. In the village of Waterford, turn left on 8th Street, then left on Washington Avenue. Turn left and follow Flight Lock Road to the end. Return to Washington Avenue and proceed to a right on 6th Street. When it ends, turn left on Broad Street/Route 32 North. Turn right on 2nd Street, which crosses a bridge to Peebles Island. Reverse on 2nd Street, turn left back onto Broad Street, then turn right and follow Routes 32 and 4 North. Above Stillwater, when State Route 32 and U.S. Route 4 split, continue to follow U.S. 4 North to Whitehall.

The Iroquois gave Cohoes Falls its name, which means "falling canoe," and told stories of a chief's beloved daughter, who vanished into the mist when the canoe in which she napped slipped from its mooring and drifted perilously downstream.

LEFT: *Originally home to a state supreme court justice, Skene Manor in Whitehall is now a museum and tearoom.*

BELOW: *The Champlain Canal, once critical to commerce, is now a scenic waterway used primarily by recreational boaters.*

The Waterford Flight of Locks was once a key piece in New York's statewide canal system.
Library of Congress

Other compelling stops are to be found along U.S. 4, which parallels the portage route between Lake Champlain and the Hudson River that was used by traders and soldiers long before Governor Clinton concocted his canal plan. Most stops tell the story of a young nation embroiled in conflict. In Stillwater, a replica of a Revolutionary War–era log blockhouse serves as a visitors' center. In Schuylerville, tours are available seasonally of the General Philip Schuyler House. Schuyler, who was relieved of command of the northern army a month before the decisive Battles of Saratoga, rebuilt his home in just twenty-nine days after it was burned down by the retreating Brits.

The towns of Fort Miller, Fort Edward, and Fort Ann are named for fortifications that were built along this strategic route during the French and Indian War. In Fort Edward, the seasonally operated Old Fort House Museum is a collection of historic structures, including the house built in 1772 by Patrick Smyth with timbers from the ruins of the fort. The home served as headquarters for both British and American officers at various times during the American Revolution; two future presidents, George Washington and James Monroe, dined together here in 1783.

Fort Edward's Union Cemetery is the burial place of Jane McCrea, a tragic figure of the Revolutionary War. The dark-haired beauty was scalped, but despite the pleas of the British officer to whom she was betrothed, General John Burgoyne refused to punish her captors lest he upset his Indian allies. Jane's story aroused antiwar sentiment in England and compelled outraged American men to enlist.

When you reach Whitehall, turn left onto Skenesborough Drive toward Skenesborough Harbor Park. When British Army Captain Philip Skene founded Skenesborough (now Whitehall) in 1759, it was the first permanent settlement on Lake Champlain. The U.S. Navy was born here in 1776 when Benedict Arnold commandeered several of Skene's merchant ships, along with his mills in Fort Ann so that he could build more. Although Arnold's fleet of sixteen boats technically suffered defeat at the Battle of Valcour Island on Lake Champlain, he succeeded in delaying the southern advance of British troops, providing the colonial army with a much-needed year to regroup before the pivotal Saratoga battles of 1777.

As you walk along the canal in Skenesborough Harbor Park, you'll encounter the 1917 canal terminal that houses the Skenesborough Museum and its collection of war and canal artifacts. Outside the museum sits the hull of the USS *Ticonderoga*, which saw action in America's victory in the Battle of Lake Champlain during the War of 1812. Across the canal is Skene Manor, an 1874 Victorian Gothic mansion constructed of local gray sandstone.

Continue to walk or drive north to Lock 12, where you'll see the one-of-a-kind Bridge Theater, a summer playhouse built on the bridge above the lock. The theater's performers are 230 miles from Broadway, but with desire, talent . . . and a boat, they could reach Manhattan without ever setting foot on land. Their dreams may not come true, but when they reach the city, they'll see that Governor DeWitt Clinton's certainly did.

SCHOHARIE COUNTY
THE POWER OF WATER

Water is the most enigmatic of elements. It sustains all life but has unparalleled capacity to destroy. It is both a barrier and a conduit. It cools and calms, yet can generate enormous energy. Frozen, flowing, falling, stagnant: in all its forms, water has been a powerful force in shaping New York's topography, economy, and history. Schoharie County, the fertile valley west of Albany tucked between the foothills of the Catskill and Adirondack Mountains, is an ideal place to observe the impact of water's inherent duality.

Humans have long endeavored to harness water, and at the outset of this drive, you'll see two successes. Since 1926, the Gilboa Dam has controlled the flow of water impounded within the six-mile Schoharie Reservoir, the northernmost collection point in New York City's supply system. At capacity, the reservoir holds 19.5 billion gallons of water vital to nine million people 110 miles away. More than eighty years ago, hundreds of residents of the original village of Gilboa, once Schoharie County's largest settlement, gave up their houses, farmlands, and church so that this flooded basin might serve their urban brethren.

North of the dam on Route 30 is the entrance to Mine Kill State Park. Known for its watery recreational opportunities, including a waterfall hiking trail and three swimming pools, the 650-acre park overlooks the fish-stocked lower reservoir of the neighboring Blenheim-Gilboa Pumped Storage Power Project. Just up the road at the New York Power Authority's Visitor Center, you'll learn how this unique hydroelectric power plant, completed in 1973, recycles water from the Schoharie Creek between two five-billion-gallon reservoirs. Water rushes from the upper reservoir down a shaft five times taller than Niagara Falls, generating as much as one million kilowatts of low-cost electricity at peak demand times. Of course, it takes energy to move this spill uphill from the lower reservoir, but this process occurs during low-demand periods, when power from other sources is inexpensive.

Ingenuity also surfaces when water is an obstacle, instead of an asset. The next landmark on the journey, on the right side of Route 30, is the Blenheim Bridge. Although it is now closed to traffic, the two-lane, 228-foot Schoharie Creek crossing was the country's longest single-span covered bridge when it was built in 1855.

As you continue north, you'll see examples of water's creative and collaborative abilities. The distinctive hill formation known as Vroman's Nose first becomes visible in Watsonville. This isolated mound of bedrock was chiseled by glaciers fifty thousand years ago. The easiest trail to the summit—just over

ROUTE 13

From Grand Gorge, follow New York State Route 30 North. Turn right onto State Route 990V to view the Gilboa Dam. Return to Route 30 North. In Schoharie, turn right on Fort Road to visit the Old Stone Fort. Return to Route 30 and continue north to a left on U.S. Route 20 West. In Esperance, turn right on Charleston Street, which becomes Conover Road. Turn right on Lape Road to visit Landis Arboretum. Return to U.S. 20 West, then follow State Route 30A South to State Route 7 West. Turn right on Caverns Road, then right on County Road 9. Turn right on Discovery Drive to Howe Caverns.

Since 1863, humans have added their own chiseled messages to the "glacial graffiti," or striae, on the summit of Vroman's Nose.

ABOVE: *The 1743 Palatine House Museum on Spring Street in Schoharie, built by Palatine German settlers as a home for their minister, is open seasonally for guided tours.*

LEFT: *The Pipe Organ is one of Howe Caverns' most distinctive rock formations, and this geologic instrument is as fascinating to hear as it is to view. The "pipes" are composed of stalagmites and stalactites that have grown together.*

Nicholas Montgomery Powers was so sure of the strength of his design for the Blenheim Bridge that when the structure was assembled over the Schoharie Creek, he sat up on the roof as the final support trestles were removed. Library of Congress

a half-mile long but steep—begins at a parking area on West Middleburgh Road. Your reward when you get to the top is a sweeping view of the abundant flood plain that beckoned first to Mohegan and Mohawk farmers, then Dutch and German Palatine settlers. Water, of course, does its most fruitful work when it collaborates with the earth and sun.

In the town of Schoharie, a few miles farther along on Route 30, you can visit working farms that continue a tradition firmly established by the mid-eighteenth century, when this region was known as the "breadbasket of the Revolution." The Old Stone Fort Museum Complex features seven historic buildings, including the 1772 Dutch Reformed Church that was stockaded to protect the local populace from British and Indian invaders, who laid to waste their crops and homes in 1780. In a letter to the Second Continental Congress, George Washington lamented, "Schoharie alone would have delivered eighty thousand bushels of grain but that fine district is now totally destroyed."

North of Schoharie, turn west onto U.S. Route 20 and head to Esperance. The George Landis Arboretum is a 200-acre testament to the enduring fertility of this region. George Landis bequeathed this property to his friend and colleague Fred Lape, whose ambition was to grow every species of woody plant that would survive here. Trails wind among the more than two thousand labeled trees and shrubs within the site's forty planted acres.

The town of Howes Cave is your final destination, and billboards may tempt you to head straight for Howe Caverns, but if you miss the Iroquois Indian Museum on the way, you may never realize that you've been driving all day on the back of a giant turtle. The museum, built in the shape of a longhouse, preserves the history and artistry of the Iroquois. Its open central stairway symbolizes Sky Woman's fall through a hole in the heavens. According to the Iroquois creation story, the earth was completely submerged, but Sky Woman was rescued by water birds and taken to Big Turtle. When Little Toad spread a mouthful of mud on turtle's back, it grew to become the North American continent.

Lester Howe must have felt a bit like Sky Woman when he first descended into the hole in the earth he discovered in 1842, with the help of his cows. On hot days, instead of seeking shade under a tree, Howe's cows headed to a spot on his neighbor's farm. Curious, Howe investigated and found the spot oddly chilly. Soon, Howe and his neighbor were spending their spare time exploring a subterranean world created over the course of six million years by a raging underground river. Howe bought the mile-and-a-half-long cave from his neighbor for $100 and began offering fifty-cent, torch-lit tours that lasted nearly ten hours.

Following the installation of electric lighting and an elevator that descends sixteen stories, Howe Caverns officially opened as a public attraction in 1929. Tours—available year-round since the cave stays a constant 52 degrees Fahrenheit—last 90 minutes and include a boat ride and opportunities to view stalagmites and stalactites, experience total darkness, and squeeze through the narrow "winding way," where you'll fully appreciate water's rock-carving capabilities. Of course, water's greatest power in New York State today may be luring tourists. Howe Caverns is the state's second most visited natural attraction—after Niagara Falls.

COOPERSTOWN TO CAZENOVIA
OUT OF THE PARK

Say "Cooperstown," and it immediately conjures up the distinctive crack of a bat connecting with a ball; the faces of icons like Babe Ruth, Hank Aaron, and Mickey Mantle; and the dreams of every kid who has ever shuffled his feet in the dirt at home plate. Cooperstown and baseball have been synonymous since June 12, 1939, when the National Baseball Hall of Fame and Museum opened its doors on Main Street. The Mills Commission, appointed in 1905 to investigate the origins of baseball, concluded two years later that the national pastime was invented by Abner Doubleday while he was a student in Cooperstown in 1839. Although the Mills Commission's findings were later discredited, this Victorian town on the shores of Otsego Lake is where support swelled for a shrine to America's game. Generations of fans have arrived here ever since to pay homage to legends and recall great moments that have left their mark not only on the sport but on the psyche of a nation.

Even non-fans will enjoy the baseball hall, but you'll miss many of the region's delights if you don't venture beyond home base. While the devout will need more time to explore the world's largest repository of baseball artifacts, casual fans can see the highlights in a morning—including the Hall of Fame Gallery, where bronze plaques commemorate the game's elite players.

That leaves ample time for a drive that showcases the rich artistic and literary legacy of an area that was home to America's first novelist long before it was home to baseball. A statue of James Fenimore Cooper stands just outside the Hall of Fame. The eleventh child of William Cooper, the land patentee for whom Cooperstown is named, was born in New Jersey. James, however, spent his childhood, young adulthood, and final years living on the banks of the sparkling lake that became the "Glimmerglass" of his *Leatherstocking Tales.*

ROUTE 14

From Cooperstown, follow New York State Route 80 East to a right on County Road 53. Turn right on Mill Road. At a stop sign, turn right onto County Road 31/Springfield Hill Road to visit Glimmerglass State Park. Turn left out of the park, and follow County Road 31 to the end. Turn left and follow U.S. Route 20 West to Cazenovia. Turn left onto State Route 13 South to visit Lorenzo State Historic Site. Backtrack on U.S. Route 20 East, and turn left onto Route 13 North to reach Chittenango Falls State Park.

ABOVE: *Notable New York Yankees artifacts in the National Baseball Hall of Fame include the first ball thrown by Governor Alfred Smith at the Yankee Stadium dedication ceremony in 1923, a pen used by Hall of Famer Joe DiMaggio to sign his $100,000 contract in 1949, and the batting helmet worn by MVP Derek Jeter in the 2000 World Series.*

ABOVE: *On a quiet autumn day, the shores of Otsego Lake in Glimmerglass State Park beckon to four-legged visitors.*

BELOW: *The Farmer's Museum was established in 1944 on lands that have been farmed since 1813, when James Fenimore Cooper owned the property.*

Chittenango Falls plummets over a series of limestone terraces in a glacier-sculpted gorge.

FINDING FAME

New York has a worldwide reputation for being ambition's destination, a place where competition thrives, heroism surges, and that certain swagger is earned through dramatic exploits. It's not surprising, then, that New York is also home to more halls of fame than you'll find anywhere else in the world.

The National Baseball Hall of Fame in Cooperstown is the best known, but within the state's borders, you'll also find museums that honor and acclaim those who have excelled in fields of endeavor as divergent as boxing and ballet, or motorsports and maple research.

As you're driving New York's byways, along them you'll find the state's twenty other international, national, and regional halls of fame:

1932 and 1980 Lake Placid Winter Olympic Museum and Hall of Fame, Lake Placid
American Maple Museum and Hall of Fame, Croghan
Catskill Fly Fishing Center and Museum/Hall of Fame, Livingston Manor
DIRT Motorsports Hall of Fame and Classic Car Museum, Weedsport
Ertegun Jazz Hall of Fame at Lincoln Center, New York City
Hall of Fame for Great Americans, Bronx
Harness Racing Museum and Hall of Fame, Goshen
International Boxing Hall of Fame, Canastota
International Women's Sports Hall of Fame, East Meadow

National Distance Running Hall of Fame, Utica
National Museum of Dance and Hall of Fame, Saratoga Springs
National Museum of Racing and Hall of Fame, Saratoga Springs
National Soccer Hall of Fame and Museum, Oneonta
National Toy Hall of Fame at Strong Museum, Rochester
National Track and Field Hall of Fame, New York City
National Women's Hall of Fame, Seneca Falls
New York State Country Music Hall of Fame, Cortland
North American Fiddlers Hall of Fame and Museum, Osceola
Professional Wrestling Hall of Fame, Schenectady
Saratoga Harness Hall of Fame and Museum, Saratoga Springs

East of the village of Cooperstown on Route 80, the Fenimore Art Museum overlooks Otsego Lake on the site of Cooper's former home. A room in the museum is devoted to artifacts associated with the prolific author, who self-published the first of his fifty-two novels in 1820 on a dare from his wife. Galleries display changing exhibits, as well as works from the museum's notable collection of American Indian, folk, and nineteenth-century American art.

Directly across the street, the Farmer's Museum is a living history museum dedicated to preserving nineteenth-century rural life. The complex of twenty-six historic buildings offers visitors an opportunity to watch costumed artisans at work, view heritage breeds of livestock and poultry, and participate in seasonal activities, from sugaring to harvesting.

Before you leave Route 80 to visit Glimmerglass State Park on the northern shores of Otsego Lake, you'll pass the home of Glimmerglass Opera. Every bit as passionate as baseball fans, opera aficionados travel each summer to see the internationally acclaimed repertory company's productions of operas old and new in this enchanting waterside setting. If eighteen holes are more likely to stir your emotions than a few high notes, you'll be pleased to know that the nearby Otsego Golf Club, one of the ten oldest courses in the country, is open to the public.

Otsego is an Iroquois word that means "meeting place by the water," and this native fishing ground still beckons to anglers, boaters, campers, and swimmers, who take advantage of the 8,000 feet of lakeshore encompassed within Glimmerglass State Park. The park is also home to Hyde Hall, an early nineteenth-century mansion regarded as one of the finest examples of neo-classical architecture in America. Even if you don't have time for a tour, be sure to stroll around the grounds, as they afford splendid views of the inspirational lake that has been called New York's Walden Pond.

Another intriguing mansion on another scenic lake awaits you at the end of this drive. To reach Cazenovia, head west on U.S. 20, America's longest road. Once known as the Great Western Turnpike, this coast-to-coast route today connects Boston, Massachusetts, and Newport, Oregon. You may pass an Amish buggy as you travel this rural segment through small towns such as Richfield Springs, home to the quirky Petrified Creatures Museum, and Madison, an antique-lover's delight.

It was a much more difficult trek in 1792 when John Lincklaen reached Cazenovia Lake and wrote in his journal, "Situation superb . . . fine land." An agent for the Holland Land Company, Lincklaen was charged with selling a tract that was part of the Amsterdam-based investment firm's purchase of 3.25 million acres in western New York. Things went swimmingly at first, and in 1807 Lincklaen built the brick mansion that stands today as part of the Lorenzo State Historic Site. His fortune changed, however, when the Erie Canal opened access to cheaper lands farther west. Still, Lincklaen's descendants managed to retain the property until 1968.

Only about sixty miles from Cooperstown, you will reach Chittenango Falls State Park, located just north of Cazenovia. A short descent to a bridge across the Chittenango Creek places you in a prime place to view the 167-foot waterfall. Close your eyes and listen. It's not the same roar professional ball players hear when they belt one over the fence, but this exhilarating sound is available to all.

Stanley Bleifeld's sculpture outside the National Baseball Hall of Fame captures a scene from the final game of the 1955 World Series, when the Brooklyn Dodgers defeated, at long last, the rival New York Yankees.

PART IV

THE ADIRONDACKS
NEW YORK'S
ORIGINAL SKYSCRAPERS

ABOVE:

A row of Adirondack chairs at Curry's Cottages on Blue Mountain Lake is a reminder that this mountainous region is as much a place for exquisite relaxation as for rugged adventure.

FACING PAGE:

At Gore Mountain, views of the snowy majesty of the Adirondack High Peaks add to the thrill of schussing down the Little Cloud ski trail.

The Adirondack Mountains in northeastern New York are composed of some of the most ancient rock on the planet—metamorphic stone formed under intense heat and pressure deep within the earth's crust more than a billion years ago. The mountains themselves, however, are relatively young. Geologists have theorized that the Adirondacks sit atop a hotspot that began to cause a gradual uplift five million years ago. In fact, the Adirondacks continue to grow, although at an infinitesimal rate of about one and a half millimeters per year. As the glaciers that covered this dome-shaped bulge in the landscape receded some ten thousand years ago, they rounded the tops of two thousand peaks, chiseled narrow mountain passages, carved out three thousand lakes and ponds, and etched thirty thousand miles of rivers and streams.

Ebenezer Emmons, state geologist for the northern New York State Geological District, named the Adirondacks in 1838 and was the first to extol their virtues as an antidote to the plagues of urban society. Verplanck Colvin was hired by the state legislature in 1872 to survey and map the Adirondack wilderness, and his eloquent pleas for preservation persuaded legislators to establish the Adirondack Forest Preserve in 1885. Colvin and others continued to lobby for additional protection, citing the region's importance as the source of the Hudson River, and in 1892, the legislature created the Adirondack Park, designating its boundaries with a blue line. Two years later, a clause was added to New York's Constitution to ensure that state land within the park "shall be forever kept as wild forest lands."

The six million-acre Adirondack Park is the largest protected area in the continental United States. Just how big is it? All of Vermont would fit inside the park's boundaries, as would Yellowstone National Park, the Florida Everglades, Glacier National Park, and the Grand Canyon National Park combined. The impact of the park's creation was even larger, as New York's pioneering model for conservation was adopted on a national scale. As president from 1901 to 1909, Theodore Roosevelt, a native New Yorker who often returned to the Adirondack wilds he cherished as a child, spearheaded preservation of 230 million acres of America's most precious natural resources within national parks, national forests, game and bird preserves, and federal reservations—that's 84,000 acres per day during his presidency.

THE ADIRONDACK COAST
CHAPTERS OF HISTORY, VOLUMES OF ADVENTURE

The Great Lakes that shape New York's northern boundaries are part of a vast inland sea that has been every bit as critical to the state's development as its Atlantic ports. Lake Champlain briefly attained "Great Lake" status in 1998, and this 121-mile ribbon of blue between two of the Northeast's most striking mountain chains (the Adirondacks and Vermont's Green Mountains) has long been strategically and economically important to the development of New York. As you set out from Rouses Point, the border town where the waters of Champlain flow into Canada's Richelieu River

ROUTE 15

From Rouses Point, follow U.S. Route 11 South to New York State Route 9B South and then take a left on Lake Shore Road. At the end, turn left on Point Au Roche Road. After viewing the Point Au Roche Lighthouse, reverse on Point Au Roche Road to a left on U.S. Route 9 South. Follow State Route 314 East to Cumberland Bay State Park. Return to U.S. 9 South, then turn left in Plattsburgh on Cumberland Avenue, which becomes City Hall Place. Turn left on Bridge Street/U.S. 9 South. In Keeseville, U.S. 9 joins State Route 22. When the two roads split, continue to follow Route 22 South to Essex.

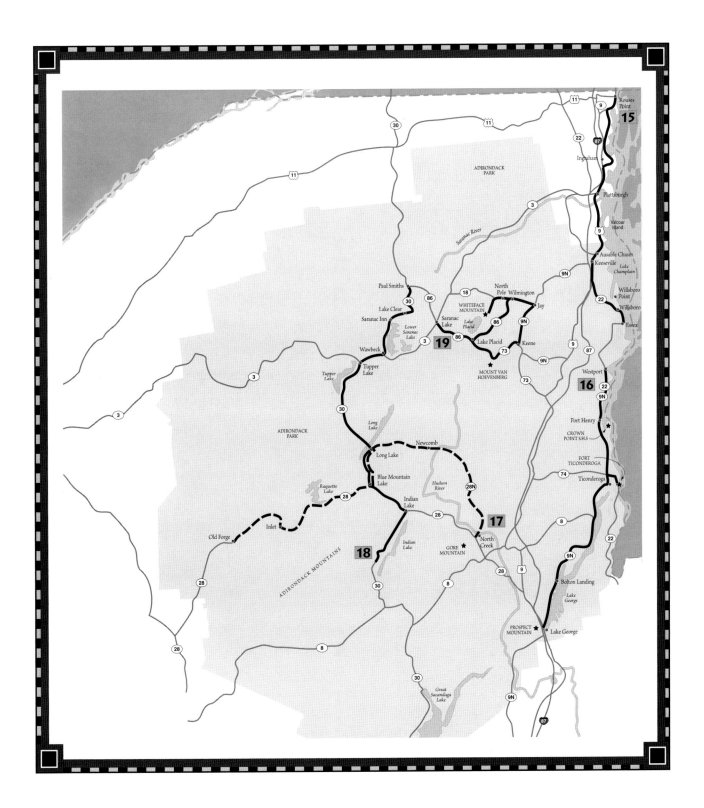

The tranquility of Lake Champlain, North America's sixth-largest freshwater lake, belies the tumult of this strategic inland waterway's early history.

A crouching Native American figure near the base of Plattsburgh's Champlain Monument gazes out over the Saranac River as it flows into Lake Champlain, a reminder of the earliest conflicts that arose as Europeans encroached on the wilderness.

With the Bluff Point Lighthouse standing sentry, Valcour Island is one of the largest islands in Lake Champlain. The island is owned by New York and located within the Adirondack Park.

The 1911 "Briarcliff" model Lozier, designed and built in Plattsburg, sold for $5,660, at a time when Cadillacs cost $750.

and on to the mighty St. Lawrence, the bucolic scenes of orchards and dairy farms, campgrounds and marinas, belie the conflict that defined Champlain's early chapters.

You'll see more boats than cars parked outside homes along Lake Shore Road, which affords scenic views of Lake Champlain to the east and the Adirondack ridge to the west. Champlain's waters teem with salmon, trout, pike, walleye, and bass, and Point Au Roche State Park is a popular spot for fishing even when the lake is frozen. Birders who follow the Lake Champlain Birding Trail—a 300-mile road tour connecting eighty-eight sites in New York and Vermont—also flock to Point Au Roche. The park has a beach, nature center, and trails for hiking and cross-country skiing. About a mile-and-a-half past the park entrance on Point Au Roche Road, you'll be able to catch a glimpse of the Point Au Roche Lighthouse on the right. Hidden behind trees and private homes, this octagonal, blue limestone tower was constructed in 1858 to warn ships away from dangerous shoals. As you continue toward Plattsburgh, you may also want to stop at Cumberland Bay State Park. A natural sand beach and campground make this seasonal park popular in the summer.

Nicknamed "the Lake City," Plattsburgh is an historic, if inelegant, urban center that has struggled to reinvent itself since the 1995 closure of its air force base. Plattsburgh played a role in every American war, from the Revolution to the Gulf War. Park your car near the Kent-DeLord House Museum on Cumberland Avenue and spend a bit of time exploring the city on foot. Start your walking tour across the street at the Champlain Monument, which is topped by a towering statue of the lake's namesake.

As you follow the Riverwalk, part of the city's well-marked, seven-mile Heritage Trail, you'll see an eagle-topped obelisk that commemorates the important victory won here by Commodore Thomas Macdonough during the War of 1812. Fought also on land, the September 11, 1814, Battle of Plattsburgh was won on the water, where an outmatched American fleet managed to inflict heavy casualties on the British aggressors, who struggled to maneuver their heavily gunned ships in the close quarters of Plattsburgh Bay. Across from the Macdonough Monument, inside the lobby of Plattsburgh City Hall, you can see the mammoth anchor from the wreck of the British flagship *Confiance*. City Hall's architect, John Russell Pope, also designed the Jefferson Memorial in Washington, D.C.

You can walk all the way to the air force base by following Plattsburgh's Heritage Trail, but if you prefer to go by car, the base's entrance is also accessible from U.S. 9. There are two public museums inside the former military installation. The Battle of Plattsburgh Interpretive Center houses artifacts and exhibits that depict the city's role in the War of 1812. The chief draw at the Champlain Valley Transportation Museum is the Lozier Gallery, which displays the luxury Lozier vehicles that were manufactured briefly in Plattsburgh at the dawn of automotive history.

Continuing south on U.S. 9, you'll come to a sign that says you have entered the Adirondack Park. Turn left into the Peru Dock boat launch site for a view of the 1874 Bluff Point Lighthouse on Valcour Island. In the mile-wide channel between the island and the shore, British warships pounded Benedict Arnold's petite naval fleet on October 11, 1776, sinking eleven of fifteen American ships during a five-hour cannon battle. It was a hollow victory for the Brits, who also suffered tremendous losses and were forced to retreat to Canada for the winter, giving the upstart Americans ample time to prepare to turn the tides a year later at the Battles of Saratoga.

At Ausable Chasm, located just a few miles farther south on U.S. 9, water is the winner in a battle of the elements that has raged for five hundred million years. Since 1870, visitors to "America's oldest natural attraction" have paid to see how the Ausable River has carved intriguing formations in ancient sandstone as it courses through the two-mile chasm. From mid May through mid October, allow at least an hour for a self-guided walking tour through the primeval forest along the chasm's rim; or if you're truly adventurous, embark on a guided rafting or weekend-evening lantern tour.

When you reach Willsboro, turn left off Route 22 onto Willsboro Point Road for a look at the Adsit Log Cabin. Built in the late 1700s, it is one of the nation's oldest log cabins still at its original location. In Essex, you'll see many examples of Federal and Greek Revival architecture. The entire hamlet is listed on the National Register of Historic Places due to its proliferation of pre–Civil War structures. By the early 1800s, Essex was a wealthy port and shipyard on Lake Champlain, but when the railroad

Tours of the Kent-DeLord House Museum, which was occupied by British officers during the Battle of Plattsburgh, offer a look at the life and possessions of three generations of a prominent nineteenth-century family.

From overlooks high above Ausable Chasm, the scenes of gouged rock walls and waterfalls are every bit as impressive as they were in 1870, when this natural attraction opened to the public.

At Fort Ticonderoga, overlooking Lake Champlain, costumed interpreters offer historical insight as they lead tours, musket-firing demonstrations, and other programs. The fort opened as a museum in 1909 and has a significant collection of military artifacts on view.

Fort William Henry was built by the British in 1755 at the southern tip of Lake George. Destroyed during the French and Indian War, it was reconstructed between 1952 and 1954 based on the original plans, found in English government archives.

reached the Champlain Valley in 1849, the hamlet's heyday abruptly ended, leaving Essex essentially stuck in the nineteenth century.

Before you close the book on your Adirondack coast journey, one more adventure awaits. Buy a round-trip ticket for Lake Champlain Transportation's twenty-minute ferry crossing from Essex to Charlotte, Vermont. If you time things right, you'll see an unforgettable Adirondack sunset on the return trip west.

WESTPORT TO LAKE GEORGE
PEACE PREVAILS

ROUTE 16

From Westport, follow New York State Routes 22 and 9N South. Turn left on Bridge Road/New York Route 910L to visit Crown Point State Historic Site. Return to Routes 22 and 9N South. Turn left and follow State Route 74 East to Fort Ticonderoga. Return to Route 9N and continue south along the western shore of Lake George. Route 9N joins U.S. Route 9 in the village of Lake George. Continue south of the village to a right on Prospect Mountain Veterans Memorial Parkway (toll) toward the summit of Prospect Mountain.

With its classic village green and Victorian inns, Westport appears at first glance to be more refined New England than rugged Adirondack. Before you leave this picturesque place on the shores of Lake Champlain, however, you'll know just where its soul lies. Most visitors arrive intending to climb high above the village to the summit of Coon Mountain for dramatic views of sparkling Champlain and Vermont's Green Mountains to the east, and the Adirondack High Peaks and verdant Champlain Valley to the west. The Nature Conservancy owns the popular, 318-acre Coon Mountain Nature Preserve, and access to the steep, mile-long summit trail is from Halds Road, a dirt road located off Lakeshore Road north of the village.

Whether or not you plan to hike, fill your water bottle in Westport. Since 1891, a pure mountain spring has provided residents with a supply of water that is so refreshing that Theodore Roosevelt had it bottled for the White House. If you have lingering doubts about Westport's Adirondack pedigree, consider this: In 1903, Westport Mountain Spring owner Thomas Lee invented a comfortable wooden chair with wide arms and a slanted back. Lee's "Westport chair" evolved to become one of the region's most recognizable symbols—the Adirondack chair.

From Westport, you'll travel south to Lake George, the Adirondacks' premier family vacationland. In the summer, visitors fight for parking spaces near the crystalline lake. During the annual winter carnival, its frozen surface is the scene of battles between teams racing outhouses across the slick ice. You'd hardly know that during the eighteenth century this was the scene of far more violent and consequential skirmishes. That is, unless you visit the ruins and re-fabrications of military fortifications located between Lakes George and Champlain.

During the French and Indian War and the American Revolution, both lakes and the overland portage route between them had immense strategic importance. The 1,360-acre Crown Point State Historic Site includes the ruins of French and British forts that were built on a hotly contested peninsula jutting into Lake Champlain. Fort St. Frederic was constructed by the French in 1734 but was demolished and abandoned in 1759 as the British advanced. The victors immediately began work on an ambitious replacement, which remained a British stronghold until after the Revolution, except for a brief period between 1775 and 1777 when it was seized by the colonists.

Crown Point, which is open seasonally, holds frequent military re-enactments and has a visitors' center that features historical exhibits. Before you depart, drive through the state-owned Crown Point Public Campground for a look at New York's most ornate lighthouse. Built in 1858, the Crown Point Lighthouse was remodeled and rededicated in 1912 as a memorial to Samuel de Champlain, the Frenchman who first explored and named the lake in 1609. Its granite base houses a bronze bust by Auguste Rodin, a gift from France.

Cheonderoga, or "place between two waters," was the Iroquois name for the land bridge between Lakes George and Champlain. The French built Fort Carillon here in 1755 and defended it fiercely, despite being outnumbered by the British four to one, during the bloody Battle of Carillon in 1758, their most significant victory of the French and Indian War. Distracted by bigger battles in Quebec, however, the French were forced to torch the fort and retreat in the face of another British attack a year later.

French General Montcalm tries to stop the brutal massacre at Fort William Henry in 1757. The Granger Collection, New York

At Fort Ticonderoga, a 2,000-acre National Historic Landmark that includes the Carillon battlefield, you can see a restoration of the British fort that was first erected in 1759. Caught off-guard by a bold, pre-dawn raid led by Benedict Arnold and Ethan Allen, the British relinquished Fort Ticonderoga in 1775. Although the rebels only held this position for two years before the British recaptured and leveled the fortress, the American presence at Ticonderoga proved an imposing obstacle in 1776 when the British opted to retreat to Canada following their victory at the Battle of Valcour.

French Jesuit missionary Isaac Jogues named it *La Lac du Saint Sacrement* in 1646, but after the French and Indian War, the English renamed Lake George for their king. As you now realize, "Warpath of Nations" is also an apt nickname for this narrow, thirty-two-mile waterway. The product of the damming of two adjacent rivers at the end of the last Ice Age, Lake George remains one of the cleanest lakes in the world due to its thickly forested and compact watershed. Because light penetrates deep into its translucent waters, the lake has a unique two-tiered fishery, with landlocked bass and pike nibbling near the surface, and salmon and lake trout inhabiting its depths.

Follow New York State Route 9N south along the lake's western bank from the serene northern end to the rollicking village of Lake George on the southern shore. In Bolton Landing, you may want to stop at Up Yonda Farm, an environmental education center with hiking trails that afford lovely lake views, or the Marcella Sembrich Opera Museum, the Metropolitan Opera diva's teaching studio until her death in 1935.

Once you reach Lake George Village, amusement parks, wax museums, arcades, miniature golf courses, shops, and restaurants will all tempt you off your "backroads" path, but if you've become captivated by tales of conflict

ABOVE: *Only ruins remain of His Majesty's Fort of Crown Point, which played a key role in Britain's efforts to wrest Canada from the French.*

RIGHT: *A sightseeing boat plies the waters of the Narrows of Lake George near Bolton Landing.*

and courage, another storied fortress awaits. Fort William Henry was built by the British in 1755 on a small rise at Lake George's southern end to guard the Great Carrying Place, the land route between the lake and the Hudson River.

You can tour the reconstructed fort, located on U.S. Route 9 just south of the village, with a British foot soldier and experience the firing of a cannon—albeit with two ounces of gunpowder rather than the two pounds used in combat. In 1757, as Britain and France sparred for supremacy in North America, the outnumbered English valiantly held the fort during a six-day siege and were allowed, finally, to surrender admirably and retreat. France's Native American allies, however, unhappy that they were denied the promised spoils of victory, pillaged the fort, massacred many, and left Fort William Henry a smoldering ruin. While historical accounts of their murderous plunder differ, James Fenimore Cooper's fictionalized version in *The Last of the Mohicans* endures. In the end, the badly depleted French troops got no further than Fort William Henry, and by 1763, the British would have their revenge—and the continent.

Within a few years of American independence, Lake George's waters were once again exceedingly calm and clear. In 1791, Thomas Jefferson wrote: "Lake George is without comparison the most beautiful water I ever saw; formed by a contour of mountains into a basin . . . finely interspersed with islands, its water limpid as crystal." From the 2,030-foot summit of Prospect Mountain, accessible via a five-and-a-half-mile toll road constructed in 1969, you'll enjoy incomparable views of this mountain-sheltered pool and appreciate how little human conflict and commercial development have altered its inherent peace.

THE HIGH PEAKS
A WILD RISE

ROUTE 17

From North Creek, follow New York State Route 28N West. In Long Lake, continue to follow Route 28N when it joins State Route 30 South. In Blue Mountain Lake, pick up State Route 28 West to Old Forge.

Theodore Roosevelt left his native New York for Washington, D.C., reluctantly. "I would a great deal rather be anything, say professor of history, than Vice President," he lamented, but his allies pushed his nomination as President William McKinley's running mate in 1900. The brash Roosevelt—who had spent his youth exploring the wilds of the Adirondacks; his college years boxing at Harvard; his young adulthood escaping the sorrow of widowhood as a cowboy herding cattle and chasing bandits in the Dakotas; his formative years as leader of the triumphant Rough Riders; and the past two years as governor of politically contentious New York—feared that the vice presidency would be interminably boring.

The Adirondack High Peaks—forty-six domed mountaintops near or over four thousand feet in elevation—are located in the remote northeastern portion of the Adirondack Park. It was here that Roosevelt sought refuge from the tedium of his new post during the summer of 1901. He was called away to Buffalo briefly, but after checking on his commander in chief, who had been shot at the Pan-American Exhibition on September 6, he returned to his family and continued his Adirondack hunting vacation. On September 13, as he descended from the summit of Mount Marcy, New York's highest peak, he received a note from the secretary of war: "The President appears to be dying."

Teddy set out on a harrowing buckboard ride over treacherous mountain roads swallowed in darkness. At the North Creek Railway Depot Museum, a plaque explains what news awaited the forty-two-year-old adventurer when he reached the train station at 5 a.m. McKinley had died at 2:15. And thus, Theodore Roosevelt became the youngest man ever to ascend to the presidency.

Your trip will be faster yet more leisurely as you retrace Roosevelt's perilous path along Route 28N, also known as the Roosevelt-Marcy Trail. But before you leave North Creek, a small ski town at the base of Gore Mountain, you may want to explore the depot museum. Exhibits tell stories of those who came by train from the 1870s until 1956, particularly Manhattanites who boarded "snow trains" in the 1930s for active weekends on the slopes. The Upper Hudson River Railroad operates scenic train rides from North Creek station seasonally. In the late summer and early fall, Northwoods Gondola Skyrides at Gore provide glorious views of the High Peaks.

Route 28N remains desolate as it climbs toward Newcomb, where the Annual Teddy Roosevelt Weekend is celebrated during the first weekend after Labor Day. Roosevelt was staying at the Tahawus Club, the Adirondacks' first sportsmen's club, in the township of Newcomb when he first learned of the attack on McKinley. Roosevelt was also a regular visitor to Newcomb's Camp Santanoni; banker Robert C. Pruyn's Adirondack great camp was the grandest yet constructed when it was built starting in 1892. The 12,900-acre property, accessible from Route 28N, was acquired by the state in 1972 and is open to the public year-round. Wagon rides and tours of historic structures are offered during the summer months. The most popular stop on Route 28N, however, is the Adirondack Park Visitor Interpretive Center in Newcomb, where exhibits offer an overview of the history and ecology of the East's largest wilderness. Three trails, including one through a two-hundred-year-old hemlock forest, allow hikers and snowshoers to probe the park.

The Adirondack Park is singular not only in its sheer enormity but also in its synthesis of state-owned and private lands. While nearly half of the six-million-acre park is public, the region is also home to about 130,000 year-round residents whose lives are entwined with the wilderness. The Adirondack Museum, located on Routes 28N and 30 overlooking Blue Mountain Lake, tells the human side of the Adirondack story. You can see the highlights of this thirty-two-acre, twenty-two-building complex in a few hours, but you could easily spend a day or more watching

Weekend visitors picnic at a lean-to near Camp Santanoni, circa 1905.
Courtesy of The Adirondack Museum

The Adirondack High Peaks have proffered solace and escape to some of the loftiest Americans.

The Adirondack Museum, in the town of Blue Mountain Lake, is home to the nation's largest inland collection of watercraft.

ABOVE: *Raquette Lake was the site of the first Adirondack great camp. Many other camps and grand resorts—rustic on the outside only—followed. Today's vacationers can still stop for a visit at Camp Sagamore, located just south of Raquette Lake on Sagamore Road.*

LEFT: *Located within the Adirondack Park, Gore Mountain caters to skiers and snowboarders with seventy-nine downhill trails and eleven lifts, including the eight-passenger, high-speed Northwoods Gondola.*

traditional artisans at work; climbing inside everything from a private luxury rail car to a rustic privy; and perusing exhibits that range from fine art to logging equipment, from horse-drawn vehicles to wooden boats. Open from Memorial Day until mid-October, the impressive museum truly connects visitors to the strength, spirit, and vision of those who have lived, worked, traveled, and played in these high peaks. You'll even see the raincoat Teddy Roosevelt wore on his historic night ride to North Creek.

In the town of Blue Mountain Lake, the Roosevelt-Marcy Trail meets the Central Adirondack Trail. As you drive west along Route 28, you'll have remarkably easy access to the scenic allure of some of the loveliest of the Adirondacks' three thousand lakes and ponds. At the turn of the twentieth century, it took more than twenty-four hours by train, carriage, and steamboat for the wealthy owners of "camps" on these lakes to travel from New

THE ADIRONDACK GREAT CAMPS

In 1869, William H. H. Murray, a Connecticut clergyman, published a book that was part travel guide, part literary narrative, and part sermon. In *Adventures in the Wilderness; or, Camp-Life in the Adirondacks*, the avid outdoorsman touted the Adirondacks' capacity not only to foster spiritual renewal but to "restore impaired health." Murray wrote, "No portion of our country surpasses, if indeed any equals, in health-giving qualities, the Adirondack Wilderness." Best of all, Murray calculated that a wellness-enhancing "month's experience among the pines" could be had for the modest sum of $125.

The book sold like hotcakes; tourists flooded the Adirondacks. Among "Murray's Fools" were many of the nation's illustrious capitalists. William West Durant, son of Union Pacific railroad tycoon Thomas Durant, created in 1877 the architectural style that would become the rage when he conceived of and built the first "great camp," Camp Pine Knot, situated along Raquette Lake's jagged, 99-mile shoreline. Inspired by the chalets he'd seen in Switzerland, and using local materials including fieldstone, notched logs, bark-covered beams, and decorative twigs, he constructed a self-sufficient compound of rustic-looking buildings that spared nothing when it came to comfort and elegance. Railroad magnate Collis P. Huntington purchased Camp Pine Knot from Durant in 1895; it is now SUNY Cortland's Camp Huntington. In 1895,

Durant completed construction of Camp Uncas for financier J. P. Morgan. Two years later, he finished Camp Sagamore on Sagamore Lake and hoped to make it his home, but financial difficulties forced him to sell the spectacular property to Alfred G. Vanderbilt in 1901.

The more than one hundred other great camps built during the Adirondacks' Gilded Age emulated Durant's techniques for blending rusticity with the epitome of luxury. White Pine Camp, built in Paul Smiths for Archibald White in 1910, served as Calvin Coolidge's "Summer White House" in 1926. In the 1920s, America's wealthiest heiress, Marjorie Merriweather Post, retreated to Camp Topridge on Upper St. Regis Lake; the estate had its own cable car to save guests the effort of walking uphill from the boat house to the main lodge. William A. Rockefeller's Wonundra, built between 1930 and 1933, was one of the last great camps constructed as the Great Depression ushered in an era of declining fortunes, during which most of these grand wilderness estates were sold off or destroyed by fire.

Wonundra is now the Point, an exclusive, eleven-room resort in Saranac Lake. More affordable lodging can be found at three other surviving great camps that welcome overnight guests: White Pine Camp and Northbrook Lodge in Paul Smiths and Camp Sagamore in Raquette Lake.

York City to their rustic yet luxurious hideaways. Blue Mountain Lake, Eagle Lake, Utowana Lake, Raquette Lake, and the Fulton Chain of Lakes still offer visitors both quiet splendor and recreational opportunities that range from paddling and fishing to seaplane rides and mailboat cruises.

Old Forge is one of seven villages within Webb, New York's largest township by area, and it offers a rich choice of activities year-round. In the winter, ski McCauley Mountain or snowmobile on a 500-mile network of groomed trails. On hot summer days, head to the Enchanted Forest Water Safari. In the summer and fall, hike the one-mile trail to the summit of Bald Mountain or hop aboard a McCauley Mountain chairlift for views of the surrounding area. Or continue on Route 28 to the village of Thendara and board the Adirondack Scenic Railroad's sightseeing train. As you ride rails once traveled by the High Peaks' elite visitors, including our twenty-sixth president, you'll have about an hour to watch the scenery roll by as you contemplate—with no sense of urgency—your life's next big adventure.

THE ADIRONDACK TRAIL
A RAT RACE ESCAPE ROUTE

The British take "holidays." In America, however, the term "vacation" came into vogue around the turn of the twentieth century and was likely first used by New York's society set, who could afford to "vacate" the city in the summer, leaving behind heat and unhealthy conditions for the cooler, cleaner air of the Adirondacks. Once seen as a cure for typhoid and consumption, the Adirondacks remain an antidote to stress, exhaustion, obesity, and other modern urban ills. The creation of the Adirondack Park, which has no gates and no admission fees, assures that your name doesn't have to be Carnegie or Rockefeller for you to realize the therapeutic benefits of a walk in the quiet woods, a paddle across a still lake, or a night under a velvety, starlit sky.

New York's Route 30 is a north-south byway that bisects the Adirondack Park and traverses some of the most tranquil and scenic locales deep within the park's interior. As you travel this segment of what is also called the Adirondack Trail, you'll discover some of the most uncrowded pockets within the park. The stretch of Route 30 between Lewey Lake and Indian Lake is the state's prime moose-viewing road. Moose began returning to New York in the 1980s after an absence of 120 years, and the population that calls this part of the Adirondacks home is now well-established.

Stop at the Tourist Information Center in the village of Indian Lake to learn about thirty hikes in the area, including the steep, 3.9-mile climb to the top of Snowy Mountain, where a 50-foot fire tower affords incredible views of blue lakes and emerald forests. In 1903 and 1908, intense fires devastated nearly one million acres of the Adirondack woodlands, prompting the construction of fifty-seven mountaintop fire towers, which were manned by fire observers from 1909 until the 1980s. The restored tower atop Snowy Mountain is one of just a handful still standing.

ROUTE 18

From Lewey Lake, follow New York State Route 30 North to Paul Smiths. Watch for turns to stay on Route 30 North: a left in Indian Lake, a right in Blue Mountain Lake, a left in Long Lake, a right in Tupper Lake, a left in Wawbeck, and a left in Lake Clear Junction.

At 3,899 feet, Snowy Mountain, which overlooks island-sprinkled Indian Lake, is higher than two rivals counted among the Adirondacks' forty-six High Peaks.

Paddling, sailing, and fishing are popular pursuits on the lake named for the isolated and imposing, conifer-cloaked Blue Mountain.

LEFT: *Inside the Natural History Museum of the Adirondacks, which opened in 2006, visitors will discover a giant glacial ice wall, a fish- and otter-inhabited river, and a twenty-foot waterfall.*

BELOW: *Situated at an oxbow of the Raquette River, the Wild Center offers a unique opportunity to view wildlife from walking trails, boardwalks, and raised observation platforms.*

Paul Smith's Hotel, shown here in 1885, was a popular Adirondacks destination for more than ninety years. Courtesy of The Adirondack Museum

As the Adirondack Trail wanders westward, spindly roadside pines bear evidence to the harsh winters here, and 3,800-foot Blue Mountain looms in your view. Island-dotted Blue Mountain Lake shares its name with a small hamlet, one of the more than one-hundred villages and towns that give the massive Adirondack Park its unique character. Route 30 turns north in Blue Mountain Lake, and although you'll drive right past the Adirondack Museum, postpone a visit for another day. While the museum is a must-see attraction, its focus is on human history and culture in the region, and your objective is to immerse yourself in the Adirondacks' natural wonders. You may, however, want to detour off Route 30 just north of the museum. Turn left onto North Point Road and drive about two and a half miles to the trailhead for Buttermilk Falls. It's a short walk to this small waterfall on the Raquette River, which teenagers use—although probably not advisably—as a waterslide.

Route 30 takes its next turn in Long Lake, where signs advertising seaplane rides may lure you to take to the skies for stunning aerial views. If you think your stomach would prefer lunch, continue on to Tupper Lake, appropriately known as the "crossroads of the Adirondacks" because Route 30 intersects with Route 3, a major east-west artery, in the center of this former lumbering town. City-weary adventurers have long found Tupper Lake a hub for outdoor pursuits including canoeing, fishing, hiking, mountain biking, cross-country skiing, and snowmobiling.

With the opening of the Natural History Museum of the Adirondacks (a.k.a. the Wild Center), Tupper Lake is also the epicenter for study, preservation, and appreciation of the extraordinary environment that has evolved among these lush peaks. Just north of Tupper Lake, turn right off Routes 30 and 3 onto Hosley Avenue, then left onto Museum Drive to visit this state-of-the-art museum. Inside the main building, exhibits depict the vast timeline of natural history in the Adirondacks and the unique ecosystem that thrives here. The mystique of the region is also vividly portrayed inside the Panoramas Theater, where nature films are shown on a fifty-foot-wide, curved screen.

The last leg of your road trip provides views of Upper Saranac Lake, Lake Clear, and finally Upper and Lower Saint Regis Lakes as you continue north to Paul Smiths. The entrance to an Adirondack Park Visitor Interpretive Center is on the left side of Route 30 just past the Route 86 junction. The center's hands-on exhibits, six interpretive trails, four back-country trails, and Native Species Butterfly House offer opportunities for close encounters with indigenous flora and fauna.

The village of Paul Smiths owes its odd name to Vermonter Apollos "Paul" Smith, who paid $300 for fifty acres on Lower Saint Regis Lake in 1858 and opened one of the Adirondacks' first wilderness resorts a year later. Three presidents—Grover Cleveland, Theodore Roosevelt, and Calvin Coolidge—were among the guests of Paul Smith's Hotel, which was legendary for its comfort and hospitality. Smith continued to accumulate real estate and sold many plots, at a tidy profit, to patrons who wanted to establish their own "great camps." After Smith's death in 1912, his son operated the hotel until it was destroyed by fire in 1930. When Phelps Smith died, he bequeathed the property and most of his fortune for the creation of a college.

While "vacation" drew luminaries like Henry Ford, Irving Berlin, and P. T. Barnum to Paul Smiths, it is now education that attracts out-of-towners to the shores of Lower Saint Regis Lake. The 14,200-acre campus of Paul Smith's College, and indeed the entire six-million-acre Adirondack Park, provide a stimulating environment for students studying ecotourism, hotel management, fishery and wildlife sciences, and forestry—and a convenient escape from anxiety come exam time.

LAKE PLACID
LAND OF MIRACLES

In 1980, the eyes of the world were on Lake Placid as Coach Herb Brooks and his young but scrappy team of amateur hockey players achieved a "Miracle on Ice," defeating the dominant Soviets in one of the most indelible and emotional victories in Olympic history. A century earlier—long before the Adirondack village of Lake Placid first hosted the world's best skiers, skaters, and bobsledders at the Third Winter Olympic Games in 1932—it was neighboring Saranac Lake that had an international reputation for working miracles.

Saranac Lake was a backwoods community inhabited by trappers, sporting guides, and lumbermen when twenty-five-year-old Edward Livingston Trudeau came north to the mountains to die. As a teen, the future doctor had cared for his older brother, James, who succumbed to tuberculosis in just three months. Believing his own tuberculosis diagnosis to be a death sentence, Edward wished to spend his final days amid the great forest he loved. After summering at Paul Smith's Hotel in 1873, he returned the next summer, and the next. In 1876, he moved his young family to Saranac Lake, and by 1880, he was strong, healthy, and ready to spend the next thirty-five years conducting pioneering tuberculosis research at his Saranac Laboratory and caring for the desperate thousands who flocked to his Adirondack Cottage Sanitarium to "take the cure."

ROUTE 19

From Saranac Lake, follow New York State Route 86 East through Lake Placid to a left turn in Wilmington onto State Route 431/Whiteface Veterans Memorial Highway (toll). After reaching the summit of Whiteface Mountain, descend via Route 431 and proceed straight onto Route 86 East. In Jay, turn right and follow State Route 9N South to Keene. Turn right and return to Lake Placid via State Route 73 West.

Wheelchair-bound Franklin Delano Roosevelt, who was governor of New York when construction began and president by the time he dedicated the Whiteface Veterans Memorial Highway in 1935, was a strong proponent of the massive undertaking, which makes Whiteface the only Adirondack High Peak that is accessible by car.

Each February in Saranac, at the oldest winter festival in the eastern United States, an enormous ice palace is built using the same ice-harvesting techniques first employed in 1898.

On some Adirondack lakes, thick blocks of ice are still harvested using traditional tools.

If you've ever dreamed of being an Olympic bobsledder, the experience of a lifetime awaits at the Mount Van Hoevenberg Olympic Sports Complex.

Little Red, the first "cure cottage," was built in 1884, and it is preserved on the grounds of Trudeau Institute on Algonquin Avenue. Author Robert Louis Stevenson was the most famous tuberculosis sufferer who benefited from a brief stay in Saranac Lake. The cottage where he spent the winter of 1887–1888, located off Pine Street on Stevenson Lane, is now a museum filled with Stevenson memorabilia. Many learned of "the Little Switzerland in the Adirondacks" and its curative atmosphere from Stevenson's writings; by the time the sanitarium closed its doors in 1954 following the discovery of a pharmaceutical cure for tuberculosis, fifteen thousand patients had been treated there. When Saranac Lake's first Winter Carnival was held in 1897, it was inspired by residents' passion for this life-giving place, even during the Adirondacks' harshest season.

Route 86 leads right through the heart of Lake Placid, the resort village on the shores of Mirror Lake, where winter and glory are synonymous. Stop at the Olympic Center, where Norwegian Sonja Henie won her second of three consecutive gold medals for figure skating in 1932, and the 1980 U.S. hockey team capped its miracle run with a win over Finland for gold. Take a self-guided tour of the center's four ice rinks, watch a skating exhibition, rent skates and go for a glide, or visit the 1932 and 1980 Lake Placid Winter Olympic Museum, which tells the Games' greatest stories through photographs, videos, and other exhibits. Adjacent to the center, you'll see the outdoor oval where Eric Heiden shattered five Olympic records on his way to an unprecedented sweep of the 1980 speed-skating races.

Only a few can aspire to such pinnacles of achievement, but this region's perpetual popularity is due in part to heights that are accessible to all. As you continue east from Lake Placid on Route 86, the first of three high points you'll encounter is High Falls Gorge. Bridges and elevated walkways enable visitors to marvel as the Ausable River's West Branch plummets 700 feet over a series of three waterfalls through an eons-old granite chasm. The attraction remains open in winter, when the frozen falls are equally stunning. At Whiteface Mountain ski area, the eight-passenger Cloudsplitter Gondola ride soars to the 3,676-foot summit of Little Whiteface, offering exhilarating views in summer and fall and access to some of the best skiing in the East when snow season arrives.

When you reach Wilmington, turn left onto Route 431, where you'll spy the entrance to Santa's Workshop in North Pole, New York. Although he's never won a medal, Santa's track record is unmatched when it comes to winter miracles, and this holiday-themed park for the pint-sized has been the red-suited hero's summer home since 1949.

Continue onward—and upward—to the top of New York's fifth-highest peak. From the tollhouse for the Whiteface Veterans Memorial Highway, open mid May through early October, you'll climb 2,300 feet in five miles. There are nine scenic overlooks along the winding drive, and after you park, you can head deep into the mountain via a 426-foot tunnel and board a handicapped-accessible elevator. This engineering marvel

takes you on a twenty-seven-story climb to the 4,867-foot summit, where a stone castle stands as a memorial to war veterans. On clear days, you can see into Vermont and Canada.

Once back in your car, descend slowly, and savor the ride as you follow the ring of roads looping back to Lake Placid. From Jay to Keene, Route 9N clings to the banks of the Ausable River's East Branch, which flows toward its meeting with the West Branch for a final sprint to Lake Champlain. In Keene, you'll pick up Route 73, the High Peaks Scenic Byway, and hug sheer cliffs as you navigate a narrow passage along Cascade Brook. If that doesn't pump up your adrenaline, rocketing down the 1980 Olympic bobsled run at Mount Van Hoevenberg surely will; wheels keep the bobsleds running in the summer. You can also elevate your heart rate at the nearby Olympic Ski Jumping Complex; catch the twenty-six-story elevator to the ski jump platform or observe the aerial acrobatics of freestylers in training.

However you choose to unleash your inner Olympian, you'll hopefully feel more alive by the end of this drive. Here in these exalted peaks, history has proven that anything can happen for those who strive to be the best, who take nothing in life for granted, and who can answer sports commentator Al Michaels' famous question, "Do you believe in miracles?" with a resounding, "Yes!"

To take full advantage of the mountain air's curative properties, many structures in Saranac Lake were built with wide porches, where tuberculosis patients could recline year-round on "cure chairs." Courtesy of The Adirondack Museum

PART V

THE SEAWAY AND FINGER LAKES REGIONS A LIQUID CENTER

ABOVE:
The lawn of the Sodus Bay Lighthouse and Museum overlooks the still-operational Sodus Outer Light, set against a backdrop of Lake Ontario's rippling, blue waters.

FACING PAGE:
Lucifer Falls in Robert H. Treman State Park is the highest of twelve showering chutes along a three-mile glen carved by the Enfield Creek.

Central New York is known for its liquid assets. From commercial waterways to placid bays, from tumbling waterfalls to tranquil lakes, the region is defined by water in all its myriad forms. There are scenes of incomparable beauty to behold as you motor through rural river valleys, hike ancient glacier-carved gorges, stand atop fragile lakeside bluffs, or gaze out from the top of a lighthouse tower.

You'll need more than your eyes, however, to truly appreciate the liquid delights of New York's midsection. Breathe deeply as you drift along the old Erie Canal at mule speed. Listen to the restless sound of lake water lapping the shore. Feel your skin tingle as you swim beneath showery falls. Taste the sweetness of maple trees' annual gift of amber syrup. Stand atop a fortress rampart and appreciate the courage of those who defended strategic water routes. Inhale the rich fragrance of Concord grapes as they turn purple on the vine. Allow your heart to mourn for lost love as a boat whisks you to a never-inhabited island castle.

Don't be surprised if you feel both at ease and exhilarated as you immerse yourself in all that surrounds you. There's a reason the experience of feeling fully awake and aware is known as being "in the flow."

THE BLACK RIVER TRAIL
WHEN IN ROME . . .

ROUTE 20

From Erie Canal Village in Rome, follow New York State Routes 46 and 49 to Route 46 North. In Boonville, turn right onto East Schuyler Street, then left onto State Route 12 North. Turn left onto Glendale Road/County Road 32. At the end, turn left onto State Route 26 South. After visiting Whetstone Gulf State Park, reverse and follow Route 26 North to the village of Lowville, then pick up State Route 812 North to Ogdensburg. In Ogdensburg, follow State Route 68 West, watching for turns, to a right on Washington Street.

The city of Rome became the gateway to the west on July 4, 1817, when unskilled laborers turned the first shovel of earth for the construction of a cross-state canal. Rome was selected as the Erie Canal's starting point because digging could proceed west for eighty miles before a lock was required. Erie Canal Village, a living history complex, is located on the site where dreams of a navigable inland waterway first became tangible reality. Open seasonally, the village's reconstructed buildings; steam train; trio of museums devoted to canal history, cheese-making, and horse-drawn transportation; and mule-pulled boat rides along a stretch of the original canal offer visitors a taste of nineteenth-century life and commerce.

Rome is also the portal to New York's North Country for those who follow the 111-mile Black River Trail Scenic Byway. Before you head north, however, be sure to visit Fort Stanwix National Monument in Rome. Films and exhibits in the visitors' center set the stage for your tour of the reconstructed eighteenth-century fort staffed by costumed guides and artisans. The British built Fort Stanwix in 1758 to repel raids during the French and Indian War and to guard the Oneida Carrying Place, an ancient portage trail between the Mohawk River and Wood Creek that was a vital link in the route from Lake Ontario to the Atlantic Ocean. During the American Revolution, Colonists refortified this strategic post and renamed it Fort Schuyler. When the British laid siege to the fort in August of 1758, Brigadier General Nicholas Herkimer led a militia to aid the captives, but the Americans were ambushed. Herkimer was mortally wounded at the bloody Battle of Oriskany. His men propped him against a tree, where he smoked a

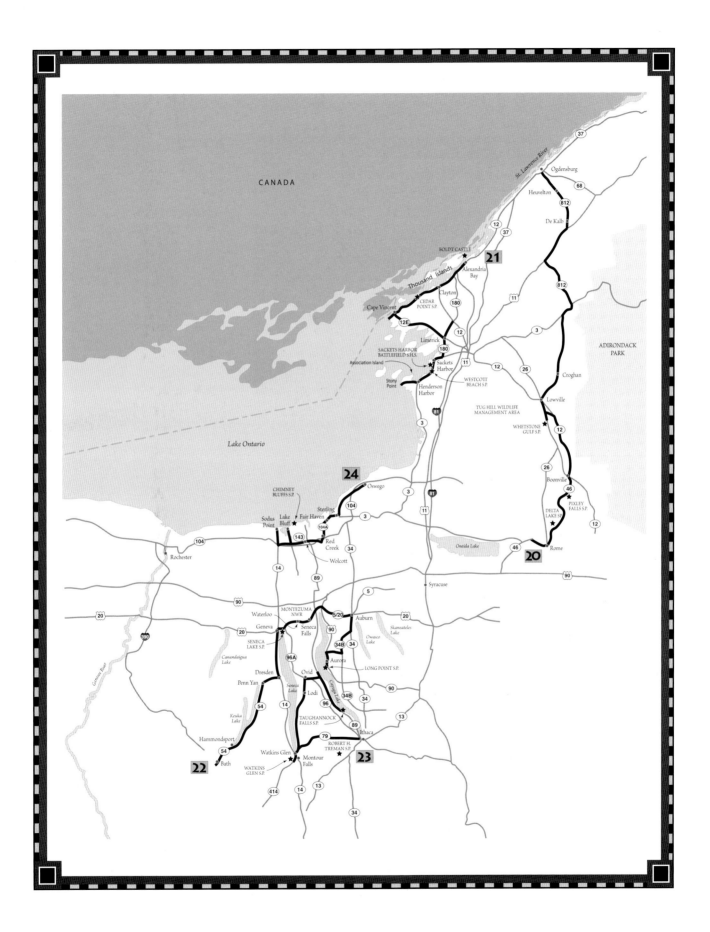

CANADA

St. Lawrence River

Ogdensburg
68
Heuvelton
812
De Kalb
37
12
37
21
BOLDT CASTLE
Alexandria Bay
Clayton
CEDAR POINT S.P.
180
812
Cape Vincent
12E
12
11
3
ADIRONDACK PARK
Limerick
180
SACKETS HARBOR BATTLEFIELD s.H.S.
Sackets Harbor
11
12
26
Croghan
Association Island
Stony Point
Henderson Harbor
WESTCOTT BEACH S.P.
Lowville
812
TUG HILL WILDLIFE MANAGEMENT AREA
WHETSTONE GULF S.P.
12
Lake Ontario
81
3
26
Boonville
46
PIXLEY FALLS S.P.
24
Oswego
3
DELTA LAKE S.P.
12
CHIMNEY BLUFFS S.P.
104
Sterling
Fair Haven
11
81
Oneida Lake
46
Rome
20
Sodus Point
Lake Bluff
104A
Red Creek
34
143
Wolcott
90
Rochester
104
14
89
Syracuse
5
90
20
MONTEZUMA NWR
Waterloo
5/20
Auburn
Skaneateles Lake
20
Geneva
20
90
Seneca Falls
SENECA LAKE S.P.
Canandaigua Lake
96A
34B
34
Owasco Lake
390
Genesee River
Dresden
Ovid
Aurora
LONG POINT S.P.
Penn Yan
Seneca Lake
Lodi
Cayuga Lake
34B
90
54
14
96
34
Keuka Lake
TAUGHANNOCK FALLS S.P.
13
Hammondsport
89
54
Ithaca
22 Bath
Watkins Glen
79
ROBERT H. TREMAN S.P.
23
WATKINS GLEN S.P.
Montour Falls
414
14
13
34

LEFT: *As winter loosens its icy grip, sap begins to flow in New York's maple-producing regions.*

BELOW: *You'll see suspendered men toiling in fields and skirted women tending to horses as you drive through the Heuvelton Amish community.*

Re-enactors at Fort Stanwix vividly portray the Revolutionary period of Rome's history.

Views of the gorge that runs through Whetstone Gulf State Park are particularly dramatic in the winter; the Tug Hill Plateau typically receives in excess of two hundred inches of snow annually as cold arctic airstreams sweep across Lake Ontario.

HERKIMER MORTALLY WOUNDED.

At the Battle of Oriskany, General Nicholas Herkimer continued to command his Continental Army troops after suffering a wound that would later kill him. The Granger Collection, New York

pipe and continued to give orders. As the confrontation raged, a sortie party from the fort raided an enemy camp, securing enough supplies to sustain the garrison until the British abandoned their futile siege after twenty days.

The Black River Trail traverses three counties as it wends its way from Rome to Ogdensburg, a port city on the St. Lawrence Seaway. As you trace the course of rock-strewn rivers that race through the narrow valley on the Adirondacks' western edge, you'll encounter one of the Northeast's most rural and remote regions. To the east lies the Tug Hill Plateau, a wooded highland the size of Rhode Island that extends north to Lake Ontario. This shale and sandstone ridge is the snowiest spot east of the Rockies.

A proliferation of public lands makes it possible for all to enjoy the recreational and scenic treasures of this unspoiled region. Delta Lake State Park, located on a peninsula that juts into the 2,560-acre Delta Reservoir, includes a beach, campground, boat launch, and hiking trails; the entrance to the park is on the left side of Route 46 just north of Rome. The reservoir was constructed in 1908 to provide water for the enlarged New York State Canal System and to alleviate spring flooding in Rome. Farther north on Route 46, just south of Boonville, Pixley Falls State Park is known for its fifty-foot waterfall, which can be viewed without a hike. It also has a cross-country ski trail along the abandoned Black River Canal, which once connected the river to the Erie Canal through a twenty-five-mile series of seventy locks.

In Boonville, the Black River Trail takes a jog and continues north along Route 12. Detour off the trail slightly to visit Whetstone Gulf State Park in Lowville. A dammed section of Whetstone Creek makes an invigorating swimming hole, and a five-mile loop trail that begins across from the beach house affords impressive views of a three-mile gorge in the eastern escarpment of the Tug Hill Plateau. You'll rejoin the Black River Trail when you turn onto Route 812 North in Lowville. Watch carefully for the Lowville Demonstration Area on the left. This former nursery, which produced 530 million seedlings between 1923 and 1971, is now an arboretum with more than 500 species of trees and shrubs. Several easy nature trails lead to interesting places within the ninety-eight-acre

CASTLE OF LOVE

Prussian immigrant George C. Boldt arrived alone in New York City at the age of thirteen and slowly worked his way up through the hospitality business. At twenty-six, he married the love of his life, fifteen-year-old Louise Keher of Philadelphia, and the two began a shared quest to develop and manage a new class of luxury hotel. George amassed a fortune, first as owner of Philadelphia's Bellevue-Stratford Hotel and then as manager of New York's Waldorf Hotel, which was later expanded to become the famous Waldorf=Astoria.

The Boldts and their two children first visited the Thousand Islands region in 1893. Two years later, Louise took deed to five-acre Hart Island, just off the shore of Alexandria Bay. The couple renamed their hideaway "Heart Island" and reconfigured its shape to more closely resemble a heart. They dismantled what was already the region's finest mansion, and in 1900, they hired 300 craftsmen to begin construction of a 6-story, 120-room, Rhineland-style castle. George spared no expense in building this home for his beloved and planned to present it to her on her birthday—Valentine's Day.

Work on the elaborate castle was nearly complete in January 1904 when a telegram arrived ordering that all construction be halted. Louise had died of a

Photo courtesy of the New York State Archives

heart attack at age forty-one. George never returned to Heart Island.

For seventy-three years, this monument to their love was ravaged by wind, water, and vandals. In 1977, the island was acquired by the Thousand Islands Bridge Authority, which has overseen restoration of the castle, Italianate gardens, and other romantic stone structures. Today, Boldt Castle is a sought-after wedding venue and a popular destination for boat tours departing from Alexandria Bay and from Canada.

property, including a collection of nesting boxes for the state's official feathered mascot—the bluebird—and a Sugar Maple orchard that is home to genetically improved versions of New York's state tree.

You'll know you're in the heart of New York's leading maple-producing region when you reach the American Maple Museum in Croghan. The three-floor museum, open only during the summer months, houses antique equipment, exhibits that explain how the labor-intensive sap-to-syrup process has evolved since Native Americans first tapped trees, and a hall of fame honoring maple innovators. The museum has a gift shop, but you can also buy a bottle of the sweet stuff directly from one of the syrup sellers you'll see as you continue along Route 812. Railroad enthusiasts will want to stop at the restored Croghan Depot, located just over the train tracks on the left, to see memorabilia from the era between 1906 and 1938 when the Lowville–Beaver River Railway transported products and passengers.

Stop next in the center of Harrisville. A tiny park tucked behind the United Methodist Church features a picnic area, a wooden bridge, and a gazebo over the syrup-colored currents of the west branch of the river Native Americans named Oswegatchie, or "black water." The Oswegatchie flows

ABOVE: *The Thousand Islands Bridge is an 8.5-mile international crossing that carries traffic over the Saint Lawrence River between Collins Landing near Alexandria Bay, New York, and Ivy Lea near Gananoque, Ontario.*

LEFT: *Looking toward New York from Canada's Skylon Tower, it is easy to understand why the Thousand Islands region attracts tourists from both sides of the Saint Lawrence Seaway.*

toward its meeting with the St. Lawrence River in Ogdensburg, and that's where you're headed, too.

Stay alert, first for turns to stay on Route 812, then for horse-drawn buggies as you travel between De Kalb and Heuvelton. The simple, agrarian nature of St. Lawrence County attracted Old Order Amish settlers from Ohio in 1974. Amish farmers still come to Heritage Cheese House to deliver their wagonloads of milk cans, but even if you're not up in time to see this morning ritual, you can visit this Heuvelton shop to buy fresh cheeses and salty, rubbery curds.

You've journeyed far from the birthplace of the Erie Canal, which accelerated America's westward expansion when it opened in 1825. In Ogdensburg, you can visit a museum dedicated to the work of a boy from the North Country who proved that the pen could be as mighty as the shovel. Frederic Remington, who was born in nearby Canton in 1861 and spent part of his youth in Ogdensburg, sparked Americans' imaginations by depicting the mythic qualities of a wild west he knew would all-too-soon vanish. His illustrations, which appeared regularly in popular magazines, captured the majestic beauty and harsh reality of the vast western expanse and celebrated the determined spirit of those who endured its perils.

The Frederic Remington Art Museum, housed in the Parish Mansion on Washington Street—where the artist's widow, Eva, lived from 1915 to 1918—showcases some of Remington's possessions, along with drawings, paintings, and bronze sculptures from all periods of his career. In 1890, the U.S. Census Bureau declared that rapid settlement had rendered the term "frontier" obsolete, and yet Remington's images still resonate today, igniting the part of our collective psyche that will always cherish the freedom to roam.

THE ST. LAWRENCE SEAWAY
A THOUSAND PIECES OF PARADISE

About 11,700 years ago, Lake Iroquois, the vast meltwater pool left behind as the last of the hulking glaciers retreated, found a new outlet to the Atlantic—the Saint Lawrence River. As Lake Ontario's predecessor began to drain, the first hunters and gatherers arrived on the shores of what the Mohawks called *Kaniatarowanenneh*, or "big waterway."

In the millennia before Jacques Cartier became the first European to sail the Saint Lawrence in 1535, the tribes that cohabited this region were often at war. According to legend, Manitou, the Great Spirit, was so distressed by the incessant fighting that he descended from the sky with a gigantic sack on his back and called his people together on the river's banks. In exchange for a promise of peace, he unwrapped for them a paradisiacal garden. Old quarrels resurfaced quickly, however, so Manitou soon returned, gathered up the garden in his bag, and returned to the heavens in a huff. As he departed, his parcel ruptured, scattering a thousand fragments into the Saint Lawrence.

Manitou has not been back, but the fabled Thousand Islands region is a paradise once again. The waters of the Saint Lawrence River and the eastern

ROUTE 21

From Alexandria Bay, follow New York State Route 12 South to Clayton, then turn right on James Street to visit the Antique Boat Museum. Backtrack on James Street and turn right onto State Route 12E. In Cape Vincent, proceed straight onto Broadway and drive out to Tibbetts Point Lighthouse on Tibbetts Point Road. Return via Broadway to Route 12E, turning right to continue south. In Limerick, turn right onto State Route 180 South. Turn right onto Old Military Road. At the end, turn right onto County Road 75, then right onto West Main Street to visit Sackets Harbor Battlefield. Follow Main Street out to a right on State Route 3 West. In Henderson Harbor, turn right onto Military Road/State Route 178.

shore of Lake Ontario, which are actually dotted with more than eighteen hundred islands, have been a peaceful international boundary for nearly two centuries. The resort community of Alexandria Bay is a perfect starting point for exploring a prime segment of the 454-mile Seaway Trail, a national scenic byway that extends west to Pennsylvania and Ohio.

From the docks at the foot of James Street—the village's shop- and restaurant-lined main thoroughfare—you'll enjoy views of Boldt Castle on Heart Island and the Sunken Rock Lighthouse, a petite tower that has marked a small but dangerous island since 1847. Boat tours offer closer access and an introduction to Heart Island lore. Each August, Alexandria Bay celebrates one of the region's most colorful characters during Bill Johnston's Pirate Days. Johnston, a Canadian expatriate, was a smuggler and renegade who burned a British ship in 1838 during his countrymen's short-lived and unsuccessful Patriot's War. The U.S. government offered a $500 reward for his capture, and after a jail stint, Johnston returned to the Thousand Islands, where he collected a $350 annual government paycheck as keeper of Rock Island Light.

Follow James Street away from the waterfront and turn left on Church Street to pick up Route 12 South to Clayton. Along the way, turn right onto Seaway Avenue to visit New York's northernmost wine producer; daily tastings are offered at Thousand Islands Winery. Back on Route 12, the entrance to Grass Point State Park is on the right. This riverside park is known for its family-friendly beach, camping, and abundant fishing, along with views of pirate Johnston's unlikely retirement lair. Now owned by the state, the grounds of the inactive lighthouse are open to the public but accessible only via private boat.

Even if you've never dreamed of owning a boat, you'll drool over the collection of hundreds of historic craft at the Antique Boat Museum in Clayton. The nine-building complex, located on the site of an old boat works and open

Commissioned in 1847 and rebuilt in 1882, Rock Island Lighthouse was one of six beacons that guided ocean-bound ships traveling from Lake Ontario.

mid May through mid October, offers opportunities to watch boat building and restoration efforts; view exhibits related to Clayton's history as a lumbering and shipbuilding port in the early 1800s; take a speedboat jaunt or a ride in a skiff; and marvel at the vessels that congregate each summer for the world's oldest antique boat show.

From Clayton to Cape Vincent, Route 12E parallels the indigo flow of the Saint Lawrence River, an integral component of the Saint Lawrence Seaway. This liquid highway of canals, locks, and deepened and widened river channels

The river village of Clayton is a favorite destination for boating enthusiasts, who come to tour the Antique Boat Museum or to launch their own skiffs.

The owners of Cape Vincent's grandest homes have enviable views of the junction of Lake Ontario and the Saint Lawrence River.

Robert G. Wehle State Park offers unparalleled vistas from a 17,000-foot stretch of cliff overlooking Lake Ontario.

links Lake Superior and the Atlantic Ocean. Although you won't need to stop for views, Burnham Point State Park has a boat dock and picnic grounds. Cedar Point State Park, established in 1897 and one of New York's oldest parks, is a good place for swimming, boating, fishing, and watching seaworthy vessels go by.

In Cape Vincent, the mighty river and Great Lake Ontario meet. The only auto ferry crossing the Saint Lawrence to Canada operates from Cape Vincent, a town with a strong French heritage. Bill Johnston would not be the Thousand Islands' most notorious retiree had Napoleon Bonaparte ever escaped to live in the house that was constructed for him in Cape Vincent. Napoleon's brother and other supporters, who had fled as the French empire collapsed, built a refuge here for the infamous emperor. Spectacular homes line Broadway, which leads to Tibbetts Point Lighthouse, a still-operational, stucco beacon built in 1854 to replace the original 1827 light. In 1984, after the lighthouse was automated, the keeper's quarters became a hostel with dorm-style and family accommodations.

You're bound next for Sackets Harbor and its War of 1812 battlefield, but you may want to stop first at the Seaway Trail Discovery Center, housed in the 1817 Union Hotel building at the intersection of Ray and West Main Streets. Hands-on exhibits introduce the architectural, agricultural, scenic, and historic highlights that motorists encounter along this nationally recognized scenic byway. At Sackets Harbor Battlefield State Historic Site, you'll learn of the village's heyday as a naval post during America's final struggle with Great Britain. Tour the Commandant's House, visit the restored navy yard, interact with re-enactors during the summer months, and walk this point of land overlooking Lake Ontario. Here, the British inflicted severe damage during an 1813 attack but were eventually repelled by the meager American troops, left vulnerable while their compatriots were off attacking Canada.

You'll pass Westcott Beach State Park as you follow Route 3 southward, and you can certainly end your day catching rays with the sunbathers or catching black bass with the anglers. If you drive on to Henderson Harbor, however, and turn right on Military Road, a choice of three backroad adventures awaits. Bear left onto Lighthouse Road, and you'll see the 1869 Stony Point Lighthouse; deactivated in 1947, it's now a cute private residence. Continue through the heart of Henderson Shores Unique Area, a reforested, 1,160-acre plot that has plentiful wildlife and unusual vegetation due to underlying limestone.

Choice two is to stay on Military Road until you reach one of New York's youngest state parks, named after the donated estate's former owner, Robert G. Wehle, a sculptor, dog breeder, conservationist, and head of the Rochester-based Genesee Brewing Company. The largely undeveloped, 1,100-acre park has ten miles of hiking and mountain biking trails.

The third option is to turn right off Military Road onto Snowshoe Road, drive over the bridge to Snowshoe Island, and stay left at the circle to cross a short causeway onto Association Island. General Electric (GE) acquired this isle in 1911 when it purchased National Electric Lamp Association, which had used the island for management meetings since 1905. GE's elite "think tank," the Elfun Society, was founded here in 1928, and in 1952, this executive retreat masqueraded as "the Meadows" in Kurt Vonnegut's first novel, *Player Piano*. After stints as a YMCA camp and training base for the 1976 U.S. Olympic Sailing Team, Association Island was abandoned for more than two decades. A private family now operates a camping resort and marina on the island. You can purchase a day pass and poke around, or consider staying the night in a rented cottage or your own RV. After all, how often do you get to sleep on a piece of paradise?

New York's Napa
Wine, Women, and Songbirds

The Finger Lakes region is best known for its wineries, and that's understandable; there are more than ninety of them. As you trace the curves of Keuka, Seneca, and Cayuga—the largest of the eleven Finger Lakes—you'll be tempted by vineyards at every turn. Each lake has a well-promoted wine trail to follow, and each member winery has its own character. Some are fledgling, others generations old; some are rustic, others quite commercial. All welcome visitors to sample the fruits of their labors.

Reds and whites aren't the only allure of these blue lakes, though, and true backroads explorers will pass the wineries by, focusing instead on the historic sights and natural wonders there to imbibe. Before the first winemaking venture was established in 1860, the shores of these deep and slender glacial lakes proved fertile ground for cultivation of both crops and ideas.

Your drive starts in Bath, where the Steuben County Fair—America's longest-running fair, held since 1819—celebrates the region's agricultural bounty each August. Apple orchards, corn fields, and dairy farms remain as much a part of the rural landscape in the Finger Lakes as vineyards. When you reach the southern tip of Keuka Lake, you'll learn that a young man's dreams of speed and flight also flourished here. The Glenn H. Curtiss Museum pays tribute to the holder of eighty-seven patents, who opened a bicycle shop in Hammondsport in 1900. Curtiss' motorcycles were the fastest on earth from 1907 until 1930, and his aviation feats included the first kilometer-long flight, design of the first plane to fly transatlantic, and invention of the seaplane.

Keuka Lake is nearly twenty miles long, and at its northern end, the village of Penn Yan boasts a classic downtown shopping district and elegant Victorian homes. Route 54 turns east from here, and you'll soon enjoy views of the deepest and most voluminous Finger Lake: 4.2-trillion-gallon Seneca Lake. Drive north along the water to Geneva, one of the

ROUTE 22

From Bath, follow New York State Route 54 North. Watch for turns to stay on Route 54 through Penn Yan. Pick up State Route 14 North to Geneva, then follow State Route 5 and U.S. Route 20 East to Auburn. Turn right on State Routes 34 and 38 South. Continue to follow Route 34 South to a right on Route 34B South. Watch for a right on Kings Corners Road. At the end, turn left on State Route 90 South. After the village of Aurora, turn right onto Lake Road to visit Long Point State Park.

RIGHT: The Finger Lakes' moderating effect on temperatures and precipitation creates a shoreline microclimate that is ideal for growing not only native grapes (Concord, Catawba, and Niagara), but also European vinifera species such as Pinot Noir, Riesling, and Cabernet Franc.

BELOW: Penn Yan, known for its Victorian homes, was incorporated in 1833; its curious name was selected because half of its settlers were Pennsylvanians, the other half Yankees.

A. E. Ted Aub's bronze sculpture re-creates the historic moment in May 1851 when Amelia Bloomer introduced Susan B. Anthony to Elizabeth Cady Stanton on a street corner in Seneca Falls.

As unsuspecting motorists whiz by on the New York State Thruway, this blue heron is sheltered and safe within the confines of the Montezuma Wildlife Refuge.

Glenn H. Curtiss flies a dirigible at Hammondsport in June 1907. The motorized dirigible was one of Curtiss' many aviation innovations. Courtesy of the Glenn H. Curtiss Museum

Northeast's prettiest small cities and home to Seneca Lake State Park, a public access point for those who want to swim in, boat on, or picnic beside the tranquil, trout-filled lake. At Geneva Medical College (now Hobart and William Smith Colleges), Elizabeth Blackwell became the nation's first woman doctor in 1849. Her fellow students voted to admit her, thinking her application was a joke. Initially ostracized, she earned the men's respect by the time she graduated first in her class.

Blackwell wasn't the only mid nineteenth-century woman who challenged traditional gender roles, as you'll learn when you reach Seneca Falls, birthplace of the women's rights movement and site of the Women's Rights National Historical Park. The visitors' center, on New York State Route 5 and U.S. 20, presents films and exhibits that tell the story of the 72-year battle for voting rights and 124-year struggle for constitutional equality. It began on July 19, 1848, when the First Women's Rights Convention convened at Wesleyan Chapel, the remains of which are adjacent to the visitors' center. Of the 300 attendees, 68 women and 32 men signed Elizabeth Cady Stanton's "Declaration of Sentiments," concurring that "all men and women are created equal." This declaration is engraved on a waterwall at the park. Tours of Stanton's home, located a short drive away on Washington Street, are also available to park visitors. The National Women's Hall of Fame, nearby on Route 5 and U.S. 20, has additional exhibits to peruse, and you may want to wander around the town of Seneca Falls a bit, particularly during the holiday season. If the town seems familiar, it may be because it inspired Frank Capra's Bedford Falls in *It's a Wonderful Life*.

About five miles east of Seneca Falls, the Montezuma National Wildlife Refuge is a wonderful place to see the songbirds and waterfowl that inhabit and visit the area—as many as two million at the height of seasonal migrations. The entrance to the refuge is on the left side of Route 5 and U.S. 20, just past the intersection with State Route 89. A 3.5-mile, 15-mile-per-hour, one-way wildlife drive through the 7,000-acre, mostly marshy tract provides amazing access to birds' nesting and resting sites. Bounded to the north by the Erie Canal and the New York State Thruway, and to the east by the Cayuga-Seneca feeder canal, this once-threatened wetland has been carefully restored since 1938. It serves as a critical habitat for wildlife, particularly migratory birds, which are best seen in mid April and late October. Bald eagles were successfully reintroduced to the refuge in 1976. Bring binoculars.

Two historic homes on South Street/Route 34 in Auburn help to tell the story of even more dramatic flight. Seward House, occupied by four generations from 1816 to 1951, was most notably the home of William H. Seward, an abolitionist, U.S. senator, and secretary of state under presidents Abraham Lincoln and Andrew Johnson. The Federal- and Tuscan-style edifice was also a stop on the Underground Railroad, which funneled many slaves to freedom. Seward is best remembered for orchestrating the purchase of Alaska from Russia, a dubious move at the time dubbed "Seward's Folly."

Few know, however, that Seward was brutally stabbed on the night of Lincoln's assassination by a co-conspirator of John Wilkes Booth, and that he provided Harriet Tubman, the most famous "conductor" on the Underground Railroad, with land for a home. He later sold her the property for a modest sum, even though the transaction was illegal. Tubman was a true guiding angel, who made nineteen trips south and led some three hundred people out of slavery. She purchased additional land adjacent to her home in Auburn for a shelter for aged blacks. The Harriet Tubman Home is now a museum dedicated to her legacy.

The final leg of your drive angles back toward the longest Finger Lake, whose Native American name, Cayuga, means "boat landing." The beach and picnic area at Long Point State Park, situated on a triangular peninsula that extends into the forty-mile lake, is a fitting place to land at the end of your day's journey. Chances are you didn't arrive here without acquiring at least one bottle of fermented grape juice, so as the sun sinks low in the sky, relax, uncork, and toast to a beautiful place and a wonderful life.

WATERFALLS OF THE FINGER LAKES
A GORGE-OUS DRIVE

Iroquois legend says that Manitou created the Finger Lakes when he pushed a piece of the heavens to earth as a reward for the bravery and devotion of his people. The region's first settlers blamed a slip of the Great Spirit's hand for the fact that there are more than five finger-like impressions in the landscape. According to geologists, however, central New

ROUTE 23

From Ithaca, follow New York State Route 13 South to State Route 327 North. When it ends, turn left onto State Route 79 West, which takes several turns en route to Watkins Glen, where it becomes State Route 414 South. In Watkins Glen, turn left and follow State Route 14 South to Watkins Glen State Park. Turn left out of the park and return via Route 14 North to Route 414 North toward Lodi. Continue to follow Route 414 North when it joins with State Route 96A North. In Ovid, turn right onto State Route 96 South. Watch for a left turn onto County Road 138. At the junction with State Route 89, head north to visit wineries or south to Taughannock Falls State Park.

A waterfall near the lower entrance to Robert H. Treman State Park provides adventurous bathers with a continuous flow of cool water in which to splash.

ABOVE: *Some segments of the well-constructed, mile-and-a-half-long, eight-hundred-stone-step Gorge Trail within Watkins Glen State Park follow footpaths first trail-blazed by Native Americans.*

LEFT: *At an impressive 215 feet, Taughannock Falls is roughly 35 feet taller than Niagara Falls.*

York's extreme makeover occurred much more slowly as the soft, sedimentary rock, formed at the bottom of an ancient tropical sea, was exposed then shaped and gouged by water and ice. Glacial action, they say, produced the deeply etched basins and the steep-walled hillsides, which are continually altered by the erosive powers of tributary streams, rushing through gorges on their descent to the outstretched mitt.

There are 150 waterfalls within a ten-mile radius of Ithaca, a college town at the southern tip of Cayuga Lake. This drive leads to several of the most picturesque cataracts, many of which are within the confines of state parks. You can see some waterfalls without leaving your car, others from easily accessible observation points, and still more if you embark on short hikes; all are at their most spectacular during the spring thaw or after substantial rainfall. You'll also have abundant opportunities to sample what's flowing at wineries along your route.

Heading south from downtown Ithaca on Route 13, turn left onto Buttermilk Falls Road to enter Buttermilk Falls State Park. The cascade visible from the parking area is the last of a series of ten distinct drops as Buttermilk Creek plunges 600 feet through a gorge. You can see the other minor waterfalls if you hike the steep Gorge Trail, one of five paths within the 792-acre park. On hot days, however, most visitors come to swim in the refreshing, lifeguard-protected natural swimming hole at the base of the falls.

There is a waterfall-fed natural pool at 1,074-acre Robert H. Treman State Park, as well, so if swimming is your thing, use that park's lower entrance off Route 327. Otherwise, continue to the upper entrance, where a half-mile hike on the Upper Loop Trail affords views of 115-foot Lucifer Falls. Near the trailhead, you can also explore an 1839 gristmill, which operated until 1917 and was the hub of the now-vanished hamlet of Enfield Falls, one of many mill towns that once thrived in the region thanks to the power of plummeting water.

You'll travel a rural stretch of Route 79 on your way to Watkins Glen at the southern end of Seneca Lake. Best known for its international auto speedway, this village is also a popular destination for those who want to experience the wild rush of waterfalls; there are nineteen of them inside Watkins Glen State Park. Journalist Morvalden Ells operated a tourist resort at the gorge from 1863 until 1906, when the state purchased the property, opening it as a public park in 1924. Even if your time or stamina is limited, be sure to walk the first segment of the Gorge Trail. You'll enter via a tunnel in the 300-foot shale and sandstone cliff, stare down into a heart-shaped plunge pool, and stand inside an eroded grotto tucked behind a glistening waterfall—all in the first minutes of your hike.

If you're game for a detour, drive south on Route 14 after leaving the park, and watch for a right turn onto North Genesee Street in Montour Falls. From the road, you'll see the 156-foot waterfall named She-Qua-Ga, or "tumbling waters," by the Seneca Indians. A sketch of the dramatic plunge resides in the Louvre in Paris, made circa 1820 by Louis Philippe, later king of France. The 1845 Greek Revival mansion beside the waterfall is reputed to be New York's most photographed house. It is now a bed and breakfast, where guests are lulled to sleep by the constant swooshing sound of the waterfall.

You can see another roadside waterfall, the 165-foot Hector Falls, surging toward Seneca Lake as you proceed north from Watkins Glen on Route 414. Nearly a dozen wineries will tempt you between here and Lodi. Whether or not you decide to stop, you'll enjoy sweeping views of carefully cultivated vineyards, many of which are more than a century old. Although grape growing has thrived in this region for generations, the proliferation of wineries is a relatively recent phenomenon. A grape price crash in the 1970s inspired many vineyard owners to look to wine-making in order to boost profits. In Lodi, turn left on West Seneca Street/County Road 136, then right on Gilbert Road, and left on Lodi Point Road to visit Lodi Point State Park. There are no waterfalls here, but you will find a peaceful marina and picnic area.

From Lodi, loop back toward Cayuga Lake and Ithaca. When you reach the junction with Route 89, a choice looms: Drive north, and more wineries await, or turn south, and more wineries await, as does the highest single-drop waterfall in the Northeast. A right turn onto Taughannock Park Road will lead you to a parking lot and viewing area overlooking Taughannock Falls. Or continue on Route 89 to the entrance for Taughannock Falls State Park in Ulysses. Inside, a flat, three-quarter-mile trail leads to a rocky amphitheater where you can watch the mist rise as this silver ribbon streaks from the sky. Even a geologist may admit it's a bit like glimpsing a scene from heaven on earth.

THE NORTH COAST
A SWELL PLACE

Picture water sloshing back and forth in a bowl, and you'll begin to understand how an enclosed body of water, such as Lake Ontario, can exhibit tide-like rises and falls. Waves that form in standing water are called seiches, and while wind and pressure changes can make these swells more dramatic, Lake Ontario has a natural, rhythmic undulation pattern that is reminiscent of ocean surf. The native Iroquois called the Great Lake *Skanadario*, or "beautiful water," and as you explore its largely rural southern shore, you'll see that the perpetual motion of this inland sea has sculpted New York State's most striking coastline.

Your starting point is Oswego, an international port city situated at the point where the Oswego River empties into Lake Ontario. Fort Ontario State Historic Site, located on East Fourth Street, has a lengthy history of guarding this strategic outlet. From mid May through mid October, visitors have an opportunity to tour the officers' quarters, enlisted men's

ROUTE 24

From Oswego, follow New York State Route 104 West to Route 104A South. In Red Creek, proceed straight onto State Route 370 East, then bear right onto Ridge Road/County Road 163. Ridge Road becomes Oswego Street. In Wolcott, turn right on Main Street/County Road 143. Turn right onto Lake Bluffs Road/County Road 154, which becomes Garner Road. Turn left on East Bay Road after Chimney Bluffs State Park. At the end of East Bay Road, reverse and continue to a right on Ridge Road/County Road 143. Turn right and follow State Route 14 North to Sodus Point.

The Oswego West Pierhead Lighthouse is visible from the ramparts of Fort Ontario. The red-roofed, white tower, built in 1934 to replace the original 1836 stone lighthouse, remains an active aid to navigation.

Actors, acrobats, jesters, and jousters entertain summer visitors at the annual Renaissance Festival in Sterling.

The climate along Lake Ontario is ideal for apple-growing, and farmstands offer juicy specimens just plucked from trees each fall.

A lighthouse museum is housed in the stone-block beacon that warned ships away from Sodus Point from 1871 until 1901.

Oswego's strategic location helped this port city to become a bustling commercial center in the nineteenth century. Library of Congress

barracks, and other structures restored to their mid-nineteenth century appearance. The first fort on the site was built by the British in 1755 during the French and Indian War. The garrison, which was destroyed and rebuilt several times, remained an important military post through World War II, when it served as America's only refugee center for Holocaust survivors.

If you're a maritime history buff, you won't want to leave Oswego without visiting the H. Lee White Marine Museum, located on West First Street. The museum exhibits nautical artifacts from the eighteenth through twentieth centuries, but the most fascinating items in its collection are the vessels moored outside, including a 1925 New York State canal barge and the U.S. Army LT-5 tugboat—a veteran of the D-day invasion of World War II.

You'll be on the Seaway Trail National Scenic Byway as you travel west from Oswego to Sterling. Best known for its Renaissance Festival, held each summer since 1976, Sterling was settled in 1805 by Peter Dumas, a Frenchman who came to America with Marquis de Lafayette to aid in the revolutionary cause. If you're game for some hiking, turn right on Center Road to visit Sterling Park and its nature center. More than fifteen miles of trails lead to intriguing sights, including a great blue heron rookery and glacially formed bluffs along a two-mile stretch of Lake Ontario. Back on Route 104A South, you'll spot the nostalgic Little Red Schoolhouse Museum. Built in 1825 and on the National Register of

Historic Sites, it is home to the Sterling Historical Society and is open to the public on a limited basis.

If you bypassed Sterling Park, you'll enjoy your first view of the eroded clay cliffs that cradle Lake Ontario as you stroll the well-groomed, 1,500-foot stretch of sand at Fair Haven Beach State Park. The entrance to this multifaceted lakefront recreation area is on the right side of Route 104A. While most visitors come for the lifeguarded beach, camping facilities, and excellent fishing, this park is also an ideal place to observe the impact of Ontario's currents on the elongated hills of glacial till, formed at the end of the last Ice Age. Known as drumlins, these rare and unusual land forms abutting the lake have endured incessant assault by wind and water, and their steep faces display nature's erratic and impressive handiwork. Look to the east as you walk along the beach or the concrete breakwater for views of Sitts Bluff.

En route to Chimney Bluffs State Park—where you can get up close to spiky, cave-riddled cliffs—you'll pass through Wolcott. Watch for Wolcott Falls Park on the right, a worthy stop for views of the small waterfall called *Ganadasgua*, or "leaping waters above the lake," by native peoples. Orchards line your route as you angle toward the Great Lake once again; the entrance to Chimney Bluffs is on the left shortly after Garner Road turns east. The soothing, ocean-like whisper of Ontario greets you as you follow a short, paved path to the lake's edge for spectacular views of the bluff and its chimney-like peaks. You may want to hike the steep, mile-long trail atop the bluff, which is particularly alluring when lined with spring wildflowers, but be sure to watch your footing. Erosion is a constant process along this high ridge, and the beach is dotted with the driftwood remains of trees that have relinquished their precarious grip on the cliff.

Enjoy one more look at Lake Ontario and its always-morphing shore-line from the park at the end of East Bay Road before you turn inland to drive around Great Sodus Bay, the south shore's largest and best protected harbor. Your final destination is Sodus Point on the bay's western tip. Settled in 1794, the village was burned to the ground by British raiders during the War of 1812, but by the mid-nineteenth century, it was a vital port for the shipment of lumber, farm commodities, and later coal from Pennsylvania when the railroad arrived. It was also a bustling tourist mecca.

A left onto Ontario Street leads to the Sodus Bay Lighthouse & Museum, where visitors can view historical exhibits, then climb the seventy-foot tower for panoramic views. Enjoy a picnic on the museum's sloping lawn, where free concerts and other outdoor events are frequently held, or continue on Route 14 to the village center. With its public beach; marinas; sport-fishing charters; bars and restaurants with rooftop decks; and waterfront rental cottages, inns, and RV sites, it's no wonder the population of Sodus Point swells to five times its usual size in summer.

PART VI

THE WESTERN DOOR
NIAGARA, CHAUTAUQUA, AND MORE

ABOVE:
A self-guided tour inside the walls of Old Fort Niagara will take you to military exhibits and re-enactments that showcase more than three centuries of military history.

FACING PAGE:
Some 75,000 gallons of water per second pour over the American Falls on the New York side of Niagara Falls, creating a thunderous roar and a scene of spellbinding proportions.

The Iroquois Confederacy was centuries old when the first Europeans made New York their home. Members of the five original nations—Mohawk, Oneida, Onondaga, Cayuga, and Seneca—referred to themselves as *Haudenosaunee*, or "people building a longhouse." The longhouse was not only a name for the elongated, one-room, bark-covered dwellings that sheltered extended families, it was also a symbol of the great peace forged among these member tribes, whose lands stretched across New York State. The Seneca, the largest of the Iroquois nations, inhabited the westernmost territory, and thus, they were known as the "Keepers of the Western Door."

Although the 1794 Treaty of Canandaigua assured that the Iroquois tribes would forever remain sovereign nations, Native American land-holdings were continually whittled away as European Americans moved westward. The completion in 1825 of the Erie Canal irrevocably altered the character of New York's frontier. Yet, while western New York is home to the state's second largest city, the region remains surprisingly rural and wild, with plenty of places that conjure images of America's other great frontier. Chautauqua is America's largest grape-growing county outside of California. Ellicottville is the "Aspen of the East," and the Genesee River gorge is the East's "Grand Canyon."

An attraction that defies comparison, however, draws more visitors to the region than any other. Niagara Falls is one of the world's wonders, a place where nature's fierce power and unmatched artistry are continually on display. Whether you follow the state's main artery, the New York State Thruway, or the backroads to the big falls, don't miss this awe-inspiring sight. In Manhattan, you'll detect New York's pulse, but as you stand above the thundering falls, or sail into their effervescent mist, you'll feel New York's heartbeat.

GENESEE COUNTRY
WATCH IT WIGGLE

You've probably never heard of LeRoy, New York, but you're almost certainly familiar with the dessert that was invented here in 1897 by carpenter and cough medicine maker Pearle B. Wait. His wife, May, gave the fruit-flavored gelatin a distinctive name, but after two years of disappointing sales, Wait sold the recipe to a neighbor, Orator Frank Woodward, for $450. Woodward's Genesee Pure Food Company already had one success—a coffee substitute called Grain-O—but it took a few years and some ingenious sales tactics to build a market for the new product. By 1902, Jell-O sales reached $250,000, and by 1909, the wiggly dessert propelled the company's revenues to over $1 million.

Jell-O was manufactured in LeRoy until 1964, and the Jell-O Museum, located on East Main Street, exhibits one hundred years of Jell-O memorabilia, from advertising art by Maxfield Parrish and Norman Rockwell to molds in every conceivable shape. Be forewarned: you may be surprised to learn how gelatin is made, but that's nothing compared to the disturbing

ROUTE 25

From LeRoy, follow New York State Route 19 South to State Route 19A South to the Portageville entrance for Letchworth State Park. (Note: When this gate is closed in the winter, turn left at the junction of State Routes 19A and 436 onto Denton Corners Road to access the park via the Castile entrance.) Follow park roads north, and exit the park via the Mount Morris entrance at the northern end. Turn right and follow State Route 36 South to State Route 408 South to the entrance for the Mount Morris Dam Visitor Center.

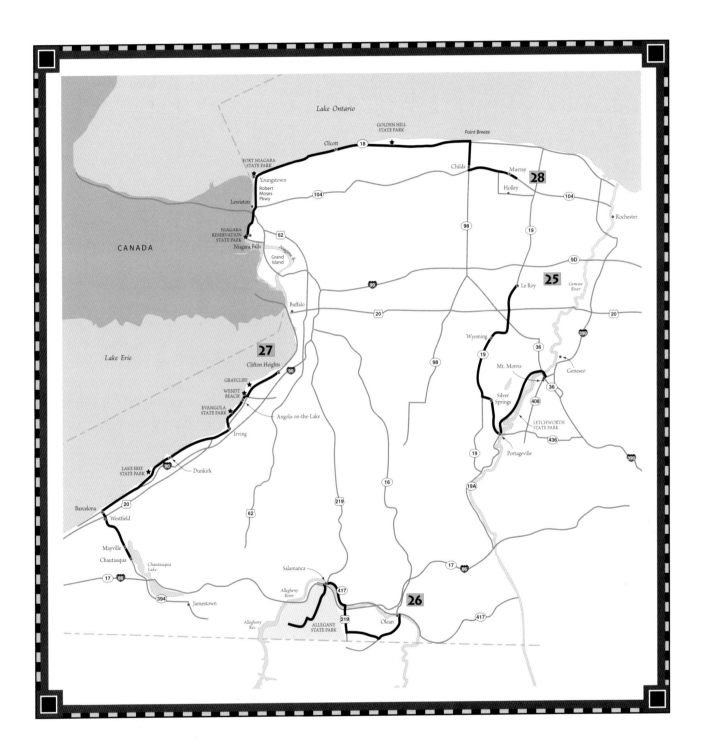

This fiberglass cow, outside the Townsend Oil Corporation in LeRoy, is decorated with a street scene.

BELOW: *Nicknamed "Gaslight Village," charming Wyoming has not only gas-fueled street lamps but more than seventy homes listed on the National Register of Historic Sites.*

In winter, intriguing icicled formations hang in the deep gorge below Letchworth State Park's Middle Falls.

The Genesee River—one of the few rivers in the United States that flows south to north—snakes and splashes its way through the seventeen-mile Letchworth State Park.

revelation that humans and lime Jell-O have identical "brain waves," as measured by an EEG machine. The LeRoy Historical Society, which operates the museum, also offers tours of the adjacent LeRoy House. Built by land agent Jacob LeRoy in the 1820s, the mansion was later home to the chancellor of Ingham University, America's first four-year college exclusively for women, established in LeRoy in 1837.

Your drive from LeRoy to Letchworth State Park traverses New York's most agrarian region. Wyoming County's forty-seven thousand cows outnumber its human population, and its milk production is unsurpassed in the state. More than a dozen maple farms produce some of New York's finest syrup. Stop to explore the village of Wyoming, where original gas-powered streetlights lend the perfect ambiance for an annual Dickens Christmas Celebration. In Silver Springs, a detour off Route 19A onto West Lake Road leads to Silver Lake State Park, a prime spot for picnicking, boating, fishing, and especially ice fishing when the shallow, three-and-a-half-mile lake freezes in the winter.

The scenery shifts instantly from bucolic to dramatic as you enter Letchworth, the 14,350-acre state park known as the Grand Canyon of the East. In 1907, wealthy businessman William Pryor Letchworth deeded to the people of New York this magnificent gift, composed of the estate he purchased in 1859 and lands he added subsequently to protect them from deforestation and development. Drivers will find frequent pull-offs overlooking the 600-foot walls of 250-million-year-old sedimentary rock that contain the winding Genesee River. Don't miss Inspiration Point, where you can view two of the three major waterfalls within the park, Upper and Middle Falls. Stop at Letchworth's former mansion home, now the Glen Iris Inn, for closer views of 107-foot Middle Falls, which is particularly impressive when illuminated at night. Descend steep stone steps for views of Lower Falls, the last cascade you'll encounter as you travel north.

The breathtaking sights visible from the road that wriggles along the gorge are reason enough to visit Letchworth, but there are also year-round recreational opportunities: hiking, biking, horseback riding, fishing, camping, swimming, snowmobiling, snowshoeing, cross-country skiing, and snow tubing. Thrill-seekers can try whitewater rafting or hot-air ballooning in this beautiful setting. The William Pryor Letchworth Museum exhibits the collection amassed by the park's benefactor, including artifacts from the region's Native American and pioneer periods and intriguing natural history items, such as a mastodon head. A preserved Seneca Council House behind the museum was the site of the last Iroquois assembly on the Genesee in 1872. Nearby, a statue marks the gravesite of Mary Jemison, who was taken captive as a teen by the Native Americans who slaughtered her family. The "white woman of the Genesee" married twice—her second husband was a Seneca chief—bore eight children, and was respected by both her adopted people and the settlers who eventually forced the Senecas onto reservations. She lived to be ninety.

Although there are plenty of reasons to stay longer at Letchworth, including elegant dining and lodging at the Glen Iris Inn, there is one more attraction that helps to tell the story of the mighty Genesee River. From 1865 to 1950, the surging river flooded the upper Genesee Valley and the city of Rochester every seven years on average, with devastating effects. Mount Morris Dam was completed by the U.S. Army Corps of Engineers in 1952. A film and exhibits at the visitors' center, and public tours of the $25 million man-made marvel, explain how the dam has saved lives and prevented $1 billion in damages to the Rochester metropolitan area. Even lime Jell-O probably knows this was a smart investment.

THE ALLEGHENY PLATEAU
ROCKS AND ROLLING RIDGES

The Delaware Indians called the river that elbows its way into southwestern New York *Welhik-heny*. They had translated the original Seneca name, *Oh-yee-ho*, meaning "beautiful river." Both Native terms were adapted by European settlers; the Allegheny River, which begins as an Appalachian spring, flows westward into the Ohio River. Allegheny is also the name of the northernmost Appalachian Plateau, a densely forested upland crisscrossed by streams, which shape its characteristic rounded ridges. An enormous tract of land within these lush hills is preserved inside the boundaries of Allegany State Park; New Yorkers never did agree with their Pennsylvanian neighbors on how to spell *Welhik-heny*.

The bulk of this drive explores the 65,000 acres of New York's largest state park, but there are a few sights to see before you reach Allegany. Set out south from the city of Olean for Rock City Park, a quirky, privately owned attraction that has been open to the public since 1890. From May through October, descend a crevice staircase to the hiking trail through this "city" of narrow alleyways and immense rock formations with names like Indian Face, Three Sisters, and Hamburger Rock. From atop Signal Rock, purported to be a Seneca signaling point, you'll be able to look out over one thousand square miles of enchanting scenery.

As you drive north on U.S. Route 219, you'll enter the Seneca Nation. You won't need a passport, but you may want to have your credit card ready to take advantage of tax-free gasoline prices. The Senecas were originally granted 30,469 acres of reservation land along the Allegheny River, but 10,000 acres were inadvertently flooded when the Kinzua Dam was built in 1964.

In Salamanca, the only U.S. city within the borders of another sovereign nation, turn right off State Route 417 onto Main Street to visit the Salamanca Rail Museum. In addition to the videos, photographs, and artifacts showcased inside, the free museum exhibits several historic rail cars outside. Return to Route 417 West, where you'll discover the Seneca-Iroquois National Museum just past the Route 353 junction and the Senecas' high-stakes bingo casino. Established in 1977 with settlement funds from the

ROUTE 26

From Olean, follow New York State Route 16 South. Just before the Pennsylvania border, turn right onto Nichols Run Road, which becomes Church Street. At the end, turn left onto Main Street, then right onto Bailey Drive and right onto U.S. Route 219 North. Turn left and continue to follow U.S. 219 North when it joins with State Route 417 West. When the two split, follow Route 417 West to Salamanca. After visiting the Seneca-Iroquois National Museum, backtrack on Route 417 East to a right on U.S. 219 South, which leads to the Allegany State Park entrance.

"Welcome to the Beautiful and Surreal" reads a sign greeting visitors to Olean's Rock City Park. The world's largest exposure of quartz conglomerate, or "pudding stone," was formed more than three hundred million years ago as sediment was deposited by fast-moving streams.

The Salamanca Rail Museum is housed in a meticulously restored 1912 passenger depot.

Autumn paints Allegany State Park's undulating hills in vibrant colors, and the views from Stone Tower are worth the small climb.

Kinzua Dam, the museum features a partially reconstructed longhouse, a clan animal exhibit, displays of art and handcrafted objects, and other exhibits that interpret the history and culture of this Iroquois nation.

Backtrack through Salamanca to U.S. 219 South, which leads to the northern entrance for Allegany State Park. There are two developed areas within the park—Red House and Quaker—but the vast majority remains undisturbed wilderness. Known for its four-season recreational opportunities, the park is at its most splendid when autumn paints its old-growth hardwood forests in vibrant tones of crimson, coral, and gold. Winter adventurers will find heated cabins, groomed cross-country trails, and more than ninety miles of snowmobiling. In the summer, guests hike deep into the primitive wilds; ride paved bike trails; rent paddleboats and canoes; cast their lines for bass, perch, crappies, and catfish; and nestle into their tents, RVs, cabins, or cottages at night.

Between 1933 and 1942, the Civilian Conservation Corps undertook many improvement projects within the park, including construction of three paved roads that provide drivers with access to scenic areas. You'll be on Allegany State Park (ASP) Route 1 as you enter the park; watch for a right turn for Stone Tower. From the top of this one-story structure, you'll enjoy views of the park's rolling terrain. Continue on ASP 1 to a stop sign. If you want to hike to wispy Bridal Falls, continue on ASP 1 and watch for the "#62" sign marking the quarter-mile trail. Otherwise, turn left onto ASP 2, and drive along Red House Lake. You'll eventually spot a left turn onto the loose stone and dirt road that leads to Thunder Rocks; kids love to climb these impressive boulders. At the end of ASP 2, turn right onto ASP 3, which leads to Quaker Lake, a placid pool surrounded by gentle slopes. En route to the Quaker Area and the park's western exit, you'll see Science Lake (a popular fishing hole) and the entrance to the Bear Caves Trail. Those who undertake this strenuous, four-mile trek can explore rock caverns that were once bear lairs.

Although black bears no longer inhabit these caves, they have other dens within the park. If you plan to leave your car at any time during your trip, be sure to stow any food supplies in your trunk. These bears have been observing visitors for a long time; they know how to break into vehicles, open coolers, and help themselves. The Seneca word for bear is *Nia'gwai*. The Delaware called the bear, *Maxkw*. If you spot one—even one that wandered over from the adjacent Allegheny National Forest in Pennsylvania—just shout, "bear!"

ROUTE 27

From Clifton Heights, follow New York State Route 5 West to a right turn onto Old Lake Shore Road (stretches of which are called simply Lake Shore Road). At the end, turn right and follow Route 5 West to Barcelona. Turn left on State Route 394 East to Chautauqua.

LAKES ERIE AND CHAUTAUQUA
A PLACE TO GROW

When the Erie Canal was completed in 1825, nearly all of the 2,400 residents of Buffalo turned out to applaud as a bottle of Hudson River water was poured into Lake Erie. By 1853, Buffalo's population had quadrupled, and the boomtown at the canal's western terminus has been the state's second largest city ever since. Clifton Heights is just thirteen miles south of Buffalo, but you'll soon feel a world away from that bustling metropolis. When you exit Route 5, you'll be following the westernmost segment of the 454-mile Seaway Trail National Scenic Byway, and you'll also be tracing an escape route used for centuries by those whose fortunes soared along with the "Queen City."

While most of the grand lakefront properties on Lake Shore Road remain privately owned, two welcome visitors. Stop first at Graycliff, a Frank Lloyd Wright–designed summer estate situated on a seventy-foot cliff overlooking Lake Erie. This was the third and final house that the prominent architect created for Larkin Soap Company executive Darwin D. Martin and his wife, Isabelle. Tours of the airy and bright 6,500-square-foot home, completed in 1927, highlight restoration efforts and the unique architectural aspects of the structure, which was built during Wright's transition away from the Prairie style that first earned him fame. Henry W. Wendt Jr.'s 170-acre summer residence is now Erie County's Wendt Beach Park, a romantic place for a stroll along the shallowest and warmest of the Great Lakes. Just past Wendt Beach, turn right to stay on Lake Shore Road and to discover other Lake Erie access points, including 733-acre Evangola State Park. Evangola's arc-shaped natural sand beach, nature trails, and campsites lure summer visitors, and winter's lake-effect snow woos snowmobilers and cross-country skiers.

Enticing detours abound as you continue west on Route 5 through "Grape Alley." The oldest and largest Concord grape-growing region in the world is home to member farms and the headquarters of the National Grape Cooperative, which owns Welch's.

In Irving, turn right onto Allegany Road and drive out to Sunset Bay, a lakeside cottage community that draws spring break–like crowds in the summer but suddenly quiets come September. In the postindustrial harbor city of Dunkirk, a right onto Point Drive West leads to Point Gratiot Park. Enjoy glimpses of Erie as you follow the one-way Park Drive, then exit onto Point Drive North, where you'll see the Dunkirk Lighthouse and Veterans Park Museum complex as you loop back to Route 5. The first shot of the War of 1812 was fired near where the lighthouse stands, and the first soldier to die in the Civil War, Corporal Cyrus Jones of Dunkirk, is buried on the property.

The entrance to Lake Erie State Park is on Route 5 in Brockton, and day visitors can opt to relax on the beach and listen to the lake's gentle lapping or hike scenic trails along the bluffs. During seasonal migrations, the park is a natural resting place for rare birds.

As you arrive in Barcelona, you'll see a unique lighthouse turned private residence on your right. The conical tower, built of beach stone in 1829, is the oldest Great Lakes lighthouse still standing. Deactivated in 1859, Barcelona Lighthouse was America's first public building fueled by natural gas. You may want to turn right on North Portage Road and head out to Daniel Reed Pier for a last look at Lake Erie before you turn inland on Route 394.

ABOVE: *During the fall, you can inhale the scent of ripening grapes as you drive through "Grape Alley" along the Lake Erie shore.*

The still-active 1876 Dunkirk Lighthouse and its Victorian Gothic-style keeper's quarters, which now houses military memorabilia, are open to the public on a limited basis.

The Chautauqua Institution's 1881 Athenaeum Hotel was one of the first lodging establishments to have electric lights, thanks to the son-in-law of Chautauqua co-founder Lewis Miller, Thomas Edison.

Each summer, thousands flock to the shores of Chautauqua Lake to be educated, entertained, and inspired.

You'll soon be driving along the serene shores of a smaller yet equally enchanting lake. It's worth venturing off Route 394, however, onto U.S. 20 West for a stop at New York's oldest estate winery. Established in 1961, the 200-acre Johnson Estate Winery in Westfield is one of a dozen members of the Chautauqua Lake Erie Wine Trail.

Your first glimpse of Chautauqua Lake will emerge as Route 394 brings you into the village of Mayville. At 1,308 feet above sea level, the narrow, seventeen-and-a-half-mile glacial scar is one of the highest navigable water bodies in North America. Mayville Lakeside Park, on your left, is open free to the public and offers a swimming beach, boat launch, picnic area, and playground. Each February, in conjunction with Mayville's I.C.E. Festival, four-hundred-pound blocks of lake ice are harvested to build a glistening castle in the park.

A LEGACY OF LAUGHTER

Her face has been seen by more people than the face of any other person who ever lived. Lucille Ball, the wacky redhead who won the hearts and still tickles the funny bones of audiences the world over, was born on August 6, 1911, in Jamestown, a blue-collar city near the southern tip of Chautauqua Lake. A visit to the queen of comedy's hometown is an opportunity to learn about Lucy's life, to relive the magic of television's early days, and to laugh once again at the antics of this beloved comedienne.

The Lucy-Desi Museum, located at 212 Pine Street in the heart of Jamestown, preserves the legacy of the inimitable couple behind television's most enduring show. You'll learn how Lucy and her on- and off-screen husband, Desi Arnaz, refused to compromise on their family life. Instead, they created their own production company, Desilu Productions, in California and committed episodes of *I Love Lucy* to tape at a time when most shows were broadcast live from New York. This not only preserved every memorable moment, but also made perpetual, global syndication possible. The museum features interactive exhibits, recordings, home movies, clothing, personal belongings, photos, and other memorabilia—most donated by their children, Lucie Arnaz and Desi Arnaz Jr.

Don't miss the opportunity to also tour the Desilu Playhouse, located a block away. In 2005, Jamestown became the permanent home for a traveling exhibition commemorating the fiftieth anniversary of *I Love Lucy*.

You'll see amazing reproductions of the sets of Lucy and Ricky's New York City apartment and the Beverly Palms Hollywood Hotel, view timeless black-and-white episodes of the show, and even have a chance to hawk Vitameatavegamin while reading from an unforgettable script. Devout fans will want to drive by the humble house at 69 Stewart Avenue where Lucy was born, as well as her childhood home at 59 Lucy Lane in nearby Celoron. Lake View Cemetery at 907 Lakeview Avenue in Jamestown is home to the Hunt family plot, where Lucy is buried with her parents and other ancestors.

Jamestown celebrates Lucy-Desi Days each Memorial Day weekend with celebrity appearances, film screenings, trivia contests, auctions, collectors' events, and more. The fervor that accompanies this annual fan fest is proof that Lucy will always be loved.

Summer, however, is when the Chautauqua region really shines—and swells. Though the original meaning of the Seneca word is debatable, the name Chautauqua is indelibly linked with the institution, and indeed a movement, that arose on the lake's shores. Founded in 1874 by inventor Lewis Miller and Methodist pastor John Heyl Vincent as a summer training camp for Sunday school teachers, the Chautauqua Institution's mission broadened almost immediately, and the lakeside Victorian village became a center for not only religion but also recreation, education, and the arts.

The Chautauqua Institution's Main Gate Welcome Center is on the left side of Route 394. Year-round, visitors of all faiths can stroll or bike the picturesque grounds, discovering such landmarks as the Miller Bell Tower. The Chautauqua Institution amphitheater was where Susan B. Anthony lobbied for women's suffrage and where Franklin Delano Roosevelt, one of nine U.S. presidents who have visited Chautauqua, gave his memorable "I Hate War" speech in 1936.

Access to the campus is free in the off-season and on Sundays during the nine-week summer program. When Chautauqua is in session, day visitors must purchase gate tickets, and some performances, classes, and lectures have additional admission fees. The promise of cultural immersion and spiritual and intellectual renewal attracts 150,000 visitors to Chautauqua between late June and late August. It took more than a quarter century for Buffalo's population to quadruple; Chautauqua's in-residence community grows from four hundred to seventy-five hundred each summer in a matter of days. Even a brief visit will stimulate your senses and expand your thinking, and you'll leave Chautauqua feeling energized and enlightened.

NIAGARA
NO NEED TO RUSH

There are much taller waterfalls, even in the United States. By volume of water, it only ranks sixth in the world. And yet legendary Niagara Falls is the most recognizable waterfall on the planet, a natural wonder of mythical proportions. It has been a destination for movie stars, presidents, and princesses; the ultimate challenge for tightrope walkers and barrel-donning daredevils; and a honeymoon haven for countless couples since Napoleon Bonaparte's brother, Jerome, brought his bride to the falls in 1803. Even Father Louis Hennepin, a French priest who accompanied René Robert Cavalier, Sieur de la Salle, on his explorations in 1678, gave the world an exaggerated perception of mighty Niagara Falls in the first written description of the falls' grandeur. Hennepin estimated the falls to be three times their actual height, and he claimed their "outrageous noise, more terrible than that of thunder," could be heard fifteen leagues off—that's forty-five miles.

If you travel on the nondescript New York State Thruway to Niagara Falls State Park, as most of the more than eight million annual visitors do,

ROUTE 28

From Holley, follow New York State Route 104 West to Childs. Turn right and follow State Route 98 North (watch for turns) out to Point Breeze. At the end of Route 98, turn left on Ontario Street to visit Orleans County Marine Park. Return to Route 98 and drive south to a right on State Route 18 West. Pick up the Robert B. Moses Parkway South and travel one exit to State Route 18F. After visiting Fort Niagara State Park, continue on Route 18F South through Youngstown. Watch for turns to stay on Route 18F through Lewiston. When Route 18F ends, continue south on the Robert B. Moses Parkway to Niagara Falls.

RIGHT: *This spiral staircase leads to the old lantern atop Thirty Mile Point Lighthouse in Golden Hill State Park. The light was decommissioned in 1958, and the cottage is now rented to overnight guests.*

BELOW: *A rock talus slope in Devil's Hole State Park overlooks the churning foam of the Niagara River.*

Viewed from the Canadian side, Horseshoe and American Falls are graced by an arcing rainbow, a common sight over Niagara, as sunlight mixes with the falls' fine spray.

Niagara Falls is even more mesmerizing when bathed in colored light at dusk.

In October 1901, sixty-three-year-old Annie Edson Taylor became the first person ever to go over Niagara Falls in a barrel, which she designed herself. Courtesy of the Niagara Falls (Ontario) Public Library

you won't hear even a faint rumbling when you reach exit 48A, about forty-five miles away in Pembroke. If you take the more leisurely, circuitous, and scenic route, you won't hear the percussive rush of the falls any sooner, but you *will* be treated to a stunning visual prelude.

New York's Route 104 was known as the "Honeymoon Highway" in the days before the Thruway was completed in 1960. It is also called Ridge Road because it follows the raised edge of what was once the shore of ancient Lake Iroquois, precursor to Lake Ontario. As you motor past the fields of cabbage, sprawling orchards, and kaleidoscopic flower gardens that thrive along this fertile, temperate lake plain, you may conclude that "Homegrown Highway" is the most apt nickname. Don't miss Hurd Orchards in Holley, a picture-perfect fruit and flower farm that has been operated by eight generations of the same family. Sample the farm market's products, homemade from historic and regional recipes, and head out into the orchard to pick your own fresh, sweet fruit.

Route 104 also parallels the Erie Canal, and when you reach Childs, you'll encounter an architectural form that originated in western New York. Cobblestone structures—nearly one thousand of which were built within a seventy-five mile radius of Rochester—were likely the work of stone masons in need of a new line of business after the canal was completed. While glacier-smoothed "cobbles" were freely available, the work of custom-fitting each small stone was painstaking, and by the time of the Civil War, this construction technique was largely abandoned. The Cobblestone Society Museum in Childs preserves three of these architectural masterpieces, including the oldest cobblestone church in North America, which dates to 1834 and once counted George Pullman of railroad-car fame among its parishioners.

Just west of the museum, turn right on Route 98, which leads to Orleans County Marine Park at the tip of Point Breeze, a protected harbor on Lake Ontario known for its calm waters and vivid sunsets. Chinook salmon, typically weighing thirty pounds, are the prized catch for those who depart from the marina on deep-lake fishing charters. America's Great Lakes hold about one-fifth of the world's freshwater. The outflow from Lakes Superior, Michigan, Huron, and Erie takes an incredible tumble as it descends toward Lake Ontario via the Niagara River, but as you skirt Ontario's shore, you still won't sense the tumult that lies ahead.

Route 18 is lined with apple orchards, berry patches, wineries, parks, and beaches. If you're in no rush to reach the falls, stop often. At minimum, drive through Golden Hill State Park, which lies just across the Niagara County line in the town of Barker. In addition to offering camping, fishing, boating, hiking, and picnicking opportunities, the park is home to Thirty Mile Point Lighthouse. Built in 1875, the stone beacon served to warn navigators of a rocky shoal and shifting sandbar at this spot thirty miles from the mouth of the

Niagara River. Charming Olcott Beach is another ideal place to stretch your legs. Explore the harbor town's shops and restaurants, lakeside Krull Park, and the Olcott Beach Carousel Park, where kids pay only a quarter to ride a 1928 Allan Herschell merry-go-round and several other restored rides from the 1940s.

Fort Niagara State Park and Old Fort Niagara State Historic Site are adjacent, state-owned properties located at the mouth of the Niagara River. The former is a four-season recreational facility with a beach, waterslide, swimming pools, tennis courts, hiking and cross-country ski trails, and boat launches on both the river and Lake Ontario. The latter is a centuries-old complex of fortifications. The French established Fort Conti in 1679, and the "French Castle," erected in 1726, is the oldest surviving building in the Great Lakes region. This garrison played an important role as the French, British, and later Americans struggled to control a vital access point into the heartland. Just outside the old fort, which remained an American military installation until 1963, the 1872 Fort Niagara Light is an octagonal gray stone lighthouse that now serves as a museum and gift shop; it was decommissioned in 1993.

As you head south on Route 18F, you'll be driving alongside the Niagara River, which is actually a thirty-five-mile strait joining Lakes Ontario and Erie. Along the Robert B. Moses Parkway, you'll see entrances for Devil's Hole and Whirlpool State Parks. Both offer overlooks from which to observe some of the world's wildest water and stairways that descend to the Niagara Gorge Trail along the rollicking river's edge.

Finally, you'll exit the Robert B. Moses Parkway at Prospect Street. Even after this lengthy buildup, you will be awestruck when you enter Niagara Falls State Park and set eye on the trio of waterfalls—the American and Bridal Veil Falls on the New York side and the Horseshoe Falls on the Canadian side—that comprise Niagara Falls. Established in 1885, Niagara is America's oldest state park. Its landscape was designed by Frederick Law Olmsted, who already had New York City's Central Park to his credit. Olmsted was a leader of the "Free Niagara" movement, a preservationist effort that successfully kept lands surrounding the falls from the hands of entrepreneurial speculators, ensuring that this incredible scene will always be accessible to all.

There are myriad ways to experience Niagara Falls. Going over in a barrel is not recommended; even if you join the ranks of the few who have survived this feat, you'll be fined heavily. Since 1846, when the first wood-hulled, coal-fired steamboat ferried tourists close to the falls, the Maid of the Mist has offered passengers a memorable way to appreciate the magnitude of the deluge. Boats depart from a dock inside the park, and within moments, you're close enough to feel the falls' vigorous spray, to hear their pounding roar, and to know that Father Hennepin got one thing absolutely right about Niagara: "The universe does not afford its parallel."

INDEX

ABOUT THE AUTHOR AND PHOTOGRAPHER

Photo by Al Nowak/On Location Studios

KIM KNOX BECKIUS

Photo by Meg Heilman

CARL E. HEILMAN II

Kim Knox Beckius moved to Connecticut from her native New York in 1996 but still considers the Hudson Valley "home." After graduating from F. D. Roosevelt High School in Hyde Park and completing a degree in history and communications at Marist College in Poughkeepsie, she worked in the Hudson Valley as a newspaper correspondent, a history teacher, public programs coordinator at historic Montgomery Place, and editor and spokesperson for Central Hudson Gas & Electric Corp. Since 1998, Beckius has produced a popular website devoted to travel in New England and New York State for About.com, a New York Times company. At http://gonewengland.about.com, she takes Internet users on virtual tours, offers candid reviews, and provides lively, weekly commentary on travel and events in the Northeast. Her travel writing and photography have been featured in magazines and on several other travel-related websites. Beckius is the author of Voyageur Press' *Backroads of New England*, as well as *The Everything Family Guide to New England* and *The Everything Outdoor Wedding Book*. She is also senior writer for *Grace Ormonde Wedding Style* magazine.

Carl E. Heilman II has lived in the Adirondacks of upstate New York since 1973. He fell in love with the rugged character of the Adirondack Mountains on his first climb in the High Peaks on a wild, wintry day in early 1975 and bought his first camera soon after to photograph the spectacular landscapes he was exploring. Since then, he has been photographing the wild natural landscape, working to capture on film the grandeur of the wilderness, as well as a sense of the emotional and spiritual connection he has with nature. Heilman's award-winning photographs and panoramas have been published regionally and internationally for commercial uses and in a variety of publications including books, magazines, and calendars. His credits include: *National Geographic Adventure*, *Backpacker*, *Outside*, *Nature Conservancy*, and *Adirondack Life*. He has presented many programs throughout New York State, and his fine art prints are found in numerous collections and museum exhibits. His photography books, *Adirondacks: Views of an American Wilderness* and *The Adirondacks*, were published by Rizzoli. Heilman's New York State photography books, *Wild New York: A Celebration of Our State's Natural Beauty* and *Our New York*, were published by Voyageur Press.